Shifting African Identities

Shifting African Identities

Volume II in the Series:
IDENTITY?
Theory, Politics, History

Editors:

Simon Bekker
Martine Dodds
Meshack M. Khosa

Human Sciences Research Council
Pretoria
2001

ISBN 0-7969-1986-0

Shifting African Identities
Editors: Simon Bekker
            Martine Dodds
            Meshack M. Khosa

Design and layout: Annemarie Booyens
Cover design: Nu Dog Design

Published in South Africa by:
Human Sciences Research Council
134 Pretorius Street
Pretoria, South Africa
0001
http://www.hsrc.ac.za

Contents

List of Tables

List of Contributors

Bekker, Simon B., Department of Sociology, University of Stellenbosch, STELLENBOSCH, South Africa.

Adar, Korwa G., International Studies Unit, Department of Political Studies, Rhodes University, GRAHAMSTOWN, South Africa.

Alexander, Neville, Project for the Study of Alternative Education in South Africa, University of Cape Town, CAPE TOWN, South Africa

Biaya, Tshikala K., CODESRIA, DAKAR, Senegal.

Dodds, Martine (Editorial), Department of Sociology, University of Stellenbosch, STELLENBOSCH, South Africa.

Franchi, Vijé, University of Paris X, NANTERRE, France.

Garuba, Harry, Centre for African Studies, University of Cape Town, CAPE TOWN, South Africa

Mandaza, Ibbo, Executive Director, Southern African Regional Institute of Policy Studies, HARARE, Zimbabwe.

Mazrui, Ali A., Institute of Global Cultural Studies, Binghamton University, NEW YORK, United States of America.

Osaghae, Eghosa, E., Department of Political Studies, University of Transkei, UMTATA, South Africa.

Nzongola-Ntalaja, Georges, Washington University, MARYLAND, United States of America.

Andronikof-Sanglade, Anne, University of Paris X, NANTERRE, France.

Khosa, Meshack M., (Editorial), Democracy and Governance, Human Sciences Research Council PRETORIA, South Africa.

Preface and Acknowledgements

Three separate organisations collaborated in the production of this book: The French Institute of South Africa (IFAS), the Foundation for Global Dialogue (FGD) and the Human Sciences Research Council (HSRC). In addition, three academic bodies made important contributions both to the planning of the conference on which this book is based as well as to the editorial panel which selected conference papers for publication. These are the African Studies Association of South Africa, the African Association of Political Sciences, and the Council for the Development of Social Science Research in Africa.

The conference was held in Cape Town during the second half of 1998. Thirteen papers were delivered over a two-day period. Nine of these papers were subsequently selected and authors were requested to finalise these for publication.

The publication is situated within the field of identity politics and constitutes a second volume in a series on this subject. The first volume, entitled *Identity? Theory, Politics, History*. Volume 1 was published in 1999 by the Human Sciences Research Council and was based upon an earlier conference organised by the same three collaborating organisations. Though Volume 1 included a chapter comparing processes of identity construction in Reunion and in South Africa, its geographical focus was on South Africa. Volume 2 extends this focus to the African continent as a whole and, in one chapter, to Europeans of African descent.

The editors would like to acknowledge the contributions made both to the conference and to this publication by IFAS, FGD and the HSRC. Participants at the conference and, in particular, discussants who had had the opportunity to read the papers beforehand, added value to conference proceedings and indirectly to the final chapters that make up this book. Though their contributions remain invisible, they too deserve acknowledgement.

Simon Bekker
Stellenbosch
2001

Meshack M. Khosa
Faerie Glen
2001

Acronyms

NCNC	National Council for Nigeria and the Camerouns
NGOs	Non-government organisations
NADECO	National Democratic Coalition
UNHCR	United Nations Human Commission for Refugees
IMF	International Monetary Fund
ADFL	Alliance of Democratic Forces and Liberation
DRC	Democratic Republic of the Congo
FNLC	National Liberation Front of Congo
UNAR	Union Nationale Rwandaise
APROSOMA	Association pour La Promotion sociale de la masse
MDR-PARMEHUTU	Mouvement démocratique rwandais/Parti du mouvement de l'emanapation hutu
NRA	National Resistance Army
RPF	Rwandese Patriotic Front
OAU	Organisation of African Unity
FAR	Forces Armées Rwandaises
UPRONA	Parti de l'union et progre's national
PALIPEHUTU	Parti pour la libération du peuple hutu
FRODEBU	Front pour la democratic au Burundi
CNDD	Conseil national la défense de la démocratic
ICF	Islamic Charter Front
DUP	Democratic Union Party
SACDNU	Sudan African Closed Districts National Union
SANU	Sudan African National Union
SFP	Southern Front Party
DUP	Democratic Unionist Party
SSLM	Southern Sudan Liberation Movement
SPLA	Sudanese People's Liberation Army

SPLM	Sudan People's Liberation Movement
SSPLM	Southern Sudan People's Liberation Movement
NIF	National Islamic Front
ICFP	Islamic Charter Front Party
SPAF	Sudan People's Armed Forces
SSPLM	Southern Sudan People's Liberation Movement
NIF	National Islamic Front
ICFP	Islamic Charter Front Party
SPAF	Sudan People's Armed Forces
NDA	National Democratic Alliance
BCAF	Beja Congress Armed Forces
SAF	Sudanese Allied Forces
GDP	Gross Domestic Product
GNPOC	Greater Nile Petroleum Operating Company
NOCS	National Oil Company of Sudan
CNPC	China National Petroleum Corporation
IPC	International Petroleum Corporation
EO	Executive Outcomes
NIF	National Islamic Front
UDI	Unilateral Declaration of Independence
SADC	Southern African Development Community
COMESA	Common Market for Eastern and Southern Africa
ANC	African National Congress
NEUM	Non-European Unity Movement
PAC	Pan Africanist Congress
PANSALB	Pan South African Language Board
ECOWAS	Economic Organisation of West African States
DPLG	Department of Provincial and Local Government
HSRC	Human Sciences Research Council
CGE	Commission for Gender Equality
HRC	Human Rights Commission

Chapter 1

Identity and Ethnicity

Simon Bekker

Introduction

Some one half of the participants at the 1998 Cape Town conference on which this book is based, were South African, the other half, African scholars invited from universities and other bodies located on three continents. The intention both of that conference and of this volume is to reflect upon debates on African identities as they are interpreted by these African scholars. This perspective, moreover, is situated within the continuing ferment regarding South Africa's role—both intellectually and politically—in Africa. It is only recently that South Africa was acknowledged to have become a partner, and to have rejoined the rest of the continent in this task of recording and analysing shifts in African identities. Accordingly, conference presentations and discussions were all deeply coloured by this purpose, and chapters in this book have been written from this perspective (rather than from that of a detached, "omniscient" observer).

Analyses of ethnic and religious identities predominate; historical investigations cover the period of colonial as well as postcolonial national rule; and issues of racial domination come to the fore as the geographical focus shifts to the south of the continent. Three themes in particular preoccupied both authors and discussants and are clearly reflected in this volume, namely

- language, and its embeddedness in ethnic and religious as well as national identities, is the subject of two separate chapters and is found implicitly in all the contributions;

- Western colonial influence, and its enduring effects both on identity construction and on interpretations of these identities, is directly

1

addressed in one chapter and is also found implicitly in all the contributions; and

- the relationship between shifting African identities and conflict on the continent, or, in Mazrui's words in his magisterial closing chapter of this book, "between ethnicity, religion and the balance of unity and fragmentation in Africa", underpins the work as a whole.

An introductory South African perspective

Three general observations on the notion of ethnic identity, as it is applied within African studies, are appropriate. The first is simply that the notion is a central one when we consider the motivations and actions of people caught up in competition and in conflict. Obvious though this observation may seem, it is worth re-emphasising, since the period (in South Africa, at least) during which scholars avoided or evaded ethnic issues, is recent (Bekker, 1993).

The second observation is that there is no current elegant theory on the construction and elaboration of ethnic identities which may be applied across countries, cultures and continents. Consequently scholars tend to fall back on the political economy (on instrumental explanations) to explain ethnic conflict. As a result, they are often analytically unable to explain why particular boundaries of conflict are drawn as they are by the actors themselves (for these boundaries rarely coincide accurately with socio-economic criteria).

The third observation is simply to underline that identities—in the case of this introductory discussion, *ethnic* identities—are constructed and manipulated, not "given". Though they may often be considered and even experienced as ascribed, this does not detract from their constructed nature. For Castells (1997), for example, identity refers to "people's source of meaning and experience" and to "the process of construction of meaning on the basis of (culture)".

The interpretation of ethnic identities on the African continent has not been without controversy. The evasive attitude held by a number of scholars toward the subject has already been noted. I remember attending three conferences on ethnicity in Southern Africa in the early 1990s. At all three, I, together with almost everyone else present, felt that discussions on ethnicity, though necessary and important, were distasteful. There was something a bit unpleasant and perhaps even offensive about the subject. I also recall quoting Horowitz (1985) during a seminar at the time, and eliciting an immediate and antagonistic reaction to the quote. It read: "Ethnicity is one of those forces that is community-building in moderation, community-destroying in excess." At least in Western Europe in the 1990s, in my experience, but also in Australasia I believe, there is little such unpleasantness attached to the notion of ethnicity. The explanations offered for this offensiveness of the subject in Africa, include the following two. First, ethnicity is equated with backwardness, with the remnants of pre-modernity, with "tribalism". Accordingly, to be progressive, you need to develop a national if not a world identity. Some historians argue that African intellectuals, over the past century, have been divided into such modernists—many of whom espoused ideas of European nationalism and progress—and traditionalists, who promoted ideas of mixing African experience with foreign thought. So far, the modernists appear to have won the day, thereby entrenching negative ways of thinking about African ethnicity.

In South Africa, similar ghosts from the past and dreams of the future have emerged. Does race continue to carry deep meaning? Have the meanings attached to the ethnic and racial labels of the "old" South Africa persisted, labels such as "Zulu", or "Afrikaner" or "Coloured"? Have South Africans developed a new national identity? The implication appears to be that South Africans are able to make one choice only—to belong together to a new nation, or to remain divided by offensive cleavages inherited from an unjust past. The two positions stand in an inverse relationship to each other. If older racial and ethnic identities persist, a national identity cannot emerge and, conversely, if and when these former identities dissolve, pride in and identification with the South African nation will flourish (Bekker et al., 2000). In both the African and South African cases, this perspective obstructs the examination of new sub- or supra-national identities that may be emerging.

Tribe, as a stereotype of ethnicity in Africa—widely viewed as a Western colonial construction—is commonly conceived of as a kind of given traditional form of pre-modern society that characterised the pre-colonial past of Africa, a kind of fixed ethnicity. A number of writers who are interested in ethnicity globally have made a point that is of interest in this regard. The histories and the foundation myths of different ethnic groups—as they are defined and reinterpreted today—differ in terms of their age, or antiquity. If we think of the Japanese, the Korean and the Mongolian, or the Croat and the Slav, or the Welsh, the Scots, the Irish and the English, it is apparent that their foundation mythologies and histories cover very long periods of imagined time. In Central and Southern Africa the period of imagined time of ethnic groups, as they define themselves presently, is of significantly shorter duration. In South Africa, for instance, being Zulu, Fingo or Bhaca only makes sense in imagined historical time after the Mfecane—say 150 years ago; or being Afrikaner only makes sense over a period of less than 100 imagined years. A chapter in this volume uses a similar argument about the contemporary ethnic identities of the Hutu and the Tutsi. These interpretations appear to be related to how late European colonisation took place in most of Africa and, accordingly, to the relatively late introduction of the European-fashioned modern state (Young, 1994). So, rather than seeing Africa as having unchanging tribal identities, we have here a perspective on how recent these myths and identities are.

A third theme I want to raise is the prickly notion of "race". Ethnicity is a relational concept—it has to do with insiders and outsiders. It is often useful to speak about ranked ethnicity, where one group is perceived to be superordinate to another (as in the case of the Tutsi and the Hutu) and unranked ethnicity, where this is not perceived or experienced to be the case. In a number of chapters in this volume, race does not figure as an issue at all. In South Africa, it was important and pernicious in our *apartheid* past, and is still clearly a major issue in our present. It is self-evident that race is a ranked concept. Ought it to be analysed as a case of ranked ethnicity—with foundation mythologies and the like—which would imply that racial groupings can be compared to other ranked ethnic groups? Or should it be treated as a totally different kind of phenomenon closely linked to a

European colonial past? I believe the answer is currently of importance in Southern Africa, for if race is exceptional, the routes to regulate, if not eradicate, racial identities may well be qualitatively different from those that are intended to regulate ranked ethnicity.

The structure of this book

The succession of chapters follows a geographical trajectory from West to East and subsequently to South Africa. The next six chapters, which include two on Nigeria, one each on Congo (Kinshasa), on the Great Lakes region and on the Sudan, together with one on women of African descent in Europe, are presented as academic products that include referencing and comprehensive bibliographies.

Chapter 2 explores links between language and identity. This leads to an analysis of the influence language holds in both ethnic as well as minority relations in Nigeria. Chapters 3 and 4, which focus on Nigeria and Congo (Kinshasa) respectively, focus on social movements that intend to bypass state interventions in their communities. Accordingly the focus is on ways in which identities are employed to exit from state-civil society relations, and thereby to fashion parallel societies in these countries. Chapters 5 and 6 offer historical explanations for the rise of conflictual identity politics in the Great Lakes Region and in the Sudan. The former case focuses on the construction of ethnic identities, the latter on the construction of religious identities. In Chapter 7 the challenges of living and understanding hybrid identities is discussed. African heritage and European modernity meet in the identities constructed by second-generation French women of African descent.

Chapters 8 and 9 deal with Southern African issues and are presented as edited verbal presentations without references. Chapter 8 raises the question of the role played by divergent world-views—one of European and one of African origin—in interpretations of identities in Southern Africa, and of a Southern African identity itself. Chapter 9 discusses language identity politics in South Africa, and the gap that currently exists between formal constitutional provisions for multilingualism and an increasingly monolingual practice in the public domain.

The closing chapter draws together the various themes raised in this book and may accordingly be viewed as an elegant summary conclusion to the 1998 conference. It is fitting to observe that in this final chapter, Mazrui concludes by relating the debate on contemporary African identities to the idea of African Renaissance.

References

Bekker, S. 1993. *Ethnicity in focus: The South African case.* Durban: Indicator Press.

Bekker, S., Leidlé, A., Cornelissen, S. & Horstmeier, S. 2000. The emergence of new identities in the Western Cape. *Politikon*, 27(2):221-237.

Castells, M. 1997. *The power of identity.* Malden (USA) & Oxford (UK): Blackwell Publishers.

Horowitz, D. 1985. *Ethnic groups in conflict.* Berkeley: University of California Press.

Young, C. 1994. *The African colonial state in comparative perspective.* New Haven: Yale University Press.

Chapter 2

Language and Identity in Nigeria

Harry Garuba

Introduction

In this chapter I explore the connections between language and identity in Nigeria, with ethnicity serving as the backdrop against which these issues are examined. I begin from the position that there are local and national identities and that language variation is one of the ways in which the differences between them are highlighted. However, in Nigeria, through a curious collusion between missionaries, the colonial government and local politicians, these differences were glossed over by the creation of standard languages and the deployment of common myths of origin. Languages that were hardly mutually comprehensible were declared dialects of a common tongue, and ethnic identity became fixed on the basis of this language. Variations in identity on the basis of variations in language were foreclosed, and a national ethno-linguistic identity was imposed.

I use the examples of the three major ethnic groups—the Yoruba, Igbo and Hausa—to demonstrate that clans and communities possess a local identity which is self-generated and has a symbolic value for the people themselves. National ethno-linguistic identities were therefore constructed to dispel the pull of these more authentic local identities and to serve as tools for mobilisation in the contest for political power and the struggle over limited resources. In this process, national identities created the myth of a homogeneous whole, which was then assumed to be fixed and rendered invariable. Access to multiple identities on the basis of actual language spoken was therefore blocked.

Finally, I argue that in the areas where the minority ethnic groups live, a local "pidgin" has developed for purposes of interethnic communication and commerce. This language could have provided access to an identity not based on ethnicity. However, pidgin does not have

7

enough institutional backing to be of service as the necessary avenue to an identity not based on ethnicity and mother tongue language.

The primacy of language

Long before the postmodernist valorisation of language began, the primacy of language in human experience has never been in doubt. In social practice, language functions as a vehicle of interaction and a medium of communication, but it has always possessed an added cultural dimension, as a tool of semiotic ideology. To speak a language is not only to reach out to the other but also to declare a social bond, a sense of shared values and communal identity. Language does not only *order* experience, it also *creates* experience, and in the process sets out *what* can be experienced and *how* it can be experienced. To immerse oneself in a language is to set out the parameters and possibilities of what can be experienced within that language.

Without going as far as Lacan (1997:65) to state that "it is the world of words which creates the world of things", we can safely say that language is as much a tool of human beings as human beings are tools of language. This makes of language both a mundane and mysterious phenomenon.

Since early antiquity the adoption of a particular tongue has also been a badge of membership within a particular group, a marker of a particular identity. In this sense, language and identity have often, if not always, been coupled and conjoined. But the coupling of language and identity via ethnicity raises a host of complicated issues, some of which I hope to explore in this chapter, using the Nigerian context as an example. I take the position that there are local *and* national identities. Local identities are based, among other things, on actual language spoken (dialect, if you will), and national identities are based on a standardised version which then serves as the basis of nationally recognised ethnic identities. These language-based ethnic identities are often arbitrarily constructed and they freeze the relationship between language and ethnicity, thus "perpetuating a myth of language as a strictly bounded phenomenon and ethnic groups as culturally homogeneous" (Herbert, 1992:2). Variations in identity—on the basis of variations in actual language spoken—are thereby foreclosed and access to "new ethnicities" (Hall, 1992), on the basis of new developments and the emergence of new languages, is denied.

In the Nigerian context, where an English-based pidgin has developed in the delta areas in which several minority ethnic groups live, the possibility of the emergence of a "pan ethnic" (Erickson & Schultz, 1983) identity based on this new "language", is seriously curtailed due to lack of institutional support. Transiting from one identity to another becomes impossible within this paradigm, and the possibility of assuming multiple identities based on the ability to shift between various sites of the language continuum is similarly denied.

Language, dialect and ideology

LePage and Tabouret-Keller (1985) argue that a number of factors generally contribute to ethnicity and a shared sense of ethnic identity. Among these are: a common language and culture, a common sense of origin and self-identification within the group and ascription to it by others, and/or a sense of kinship and common inheritances. Of all these factors, the idea of a "common language" appears to me to be the most problematical, that is, if we assume that by common language we mean that when one member of the group speaks, the other will automatically understand. Ethnic identity based on mutual comprehensibility among the various groups and communities is clearly difficult to sustain, because of wide variations within some so-called dialects of a particular language. Even-Zohar (1985) lists several instances of this kind of variation in a number of European languages. Among the German dialects, for instance, a Bavarian would not automatically understand Plattdeutsch or Silesian. In Denmark's two islands and one peninsula, each with its own major dialect, people speaking Jutlandic (one of the island dialects) do not, without a preparatory education, understand Zealandic (another dialect). Even in the fairly linguistically unified space of Sweden, there are variations between the dialects of the north and south that deny access to an automatic comprehension between both. Of all the languages listed by Even-Zohar, in the Norwegian example, a combination of historical, ideological, and political factors related to the issue of national identity has created intense language conflicts, highlighting the difficulties involved in coupling language and identity in a fixed, bounded and unproblematic manner. Even-Zohar's conclusions (1985:134), spell out this absurdity in a graphic manner:

> The situation today is absolutely bewildering. Here is a nation that was to be deliberately planned, with a certain deliberately constructed identity that had to be coupled with a certain language. Since that language did not exist, they invented it. The moment they wanted to bring some peaceful harmony into that torn society, the government had no better idea than to set up a committee to make a third language, in order to give the nation a unified vehicle. But today in Norway nobody uses the "common Norwegian language," and the language conflict continues to rage with alternating intensity. Ask Norwegians how many languages they know and they will reply, "Twelve: Swedish, Danish, and ten Norwegian."

The question of language and dialect is a fairly contentious one. What constitutes a "dialect" and when does it become a "language"? In the light of the examples already cited, I take the position (along with Even-Zohar, 1985:129), that "the very term dialect is a matter of ideology, because otherwise any dialect could have been transformed into a language, or at least labelled a language." In Africa, this fact is borne out by the arbitrariness with which some languages were distinguished from others and classified accordingly, even when they were mutually comprehensible and had hardly as wide a variation as others which *were* classified together. Makoni (1996:262) affirms that, "the decision to distinguish between Zulu and Xhosa was necessitated by a desire to resolve the competing interests of missionaries". And again, that "the distinction between Kangwane Zulu and Swati was politically motivated because there are more structural similarities between the two than between, let us say, urban and rural Zulu."

Harries (1994:216) describes how a group of Swiss missionaries working in Southern Mozambique and Northern South Africa created a standardised Tsonga by reordering and rearranging some linguistic signs in the dialect of the people. In fact Louw (1983:374) also describes how the missionary groups prevented the development of a standard position for Xhosa and Zulu.

What these instances prove is that the decision to label a particular tongue a "language" or a "dialect" involves several considerations centred on interests that are both semiotic and ideological. Again, as we have seen, some of these so-called "languages" are artificial constructions which acquire legitimacy from the power of the *naming* or *labelling* interest group, rather than from the *named* or *labelled*.

Ethnos, language and identity

In Nigeria there are over 400 languages spoken. Of these, three are considered "major languages", while all the others are considered "minor" or "minority" languages. By Nigerian juridical and constitutional definition, Hausa, Yoruba, and Igbo are designated major languages while the over 400 others spoken in the country are seen as minority languages. The terms "majority" and "minority", in Nigeria, also translate directly to the distribution of political and socio-economic power and status. Belonging to a majority language group means having relatively more power and status than belonging to a minority group. In a situation of intense socio-economic and political competition over the distribution of power and resources, these terms become heavily invested with semiotic and symbolic value.

As we have seen, the coupling of *ethnos* and language, and therefore also "identity", is not as "natural" as it may initially appear when these concepts are deployed. In Nigeria, as in other parts of the world, various interest and power groups were actively involved in the construction of standard languages and identities into which various peoples and communities were then boxed. To quote Makoni (1996:262): "In spite of the arbitrariness with which standard languages were created, they were expected to 'reflect ethnic identity,' with language and ethnicity being seen as a "bounded, boxing-in and homogenising phenomenon".

The fiction of linguistic homogeneity has been actively sustained at the national level by eroding local peculiarities of speech and dialect, that are not only discouraged but also denigrated as examples of uncultured and uneducated speech habits. "Tribal laagers" as Maake (1994:13) calls them, are thus created, and individuals and communities are coerced or manoeuvred into submitting to their classificatory authority.

In northern Nigeria, for example, where Hausa is the major language, other minority groups are expected to adopt and speak it because of the power and status conferred upon it. In the early 19th century, when the Fulani jihadists overran northern Nigeria, the conquering Islamists did a curious thing: instead of imposing their own Fulfude language on the entire population, they adopted Hausa, a local language, as the *lingua franca* and medium of communication throughout the Caliphate which they established. Minority languages were effectively marginalised and a new ethno-linguistic identity was created from a coupling of the power of the conquerors with the language of the conquered. In this manner, the Hausa/Fulani oligarchy was established, which has dominated the region for almost 200 years. Local identities were suppressed by a combination of the power of language and religion. When the British colonists took over, the system of indirect rule which they had instituted, promoted this identity through their language and bureaucratic policies and practices, which endorsed and reinforced it. The Kano dialect of Hausa was standardised and adopted as the "officially recognised" version.

There were at least two identity positions mobilised by the jihadists in their campaigns of conquest. The *mallams* and the *fulani-gida* who started the holy war, were an educated minority. Islam was the over-arching identity which served as the vehicle of mobilisation for communities which were not Fulfude-speaking. In short, religion was employed to mobilise the Hausa-speaking majority and the other communities. The *bororo* (the cattle fulani), however, who constituted the majority of the Fulani people, were mobilised to fight on the basis of linguistic identity.[1]

The jihadists encountered no major problems in shifting between various identity positions, because during this pre-colonial period ethno-linguistic identities of the sort we now know, were virtually non-existent. Among the Hausa-speaking peoples, identity was largely town/community based (i.e. local identities). Rather than Hausa, people saw themselves as *Ba Kano* or *Ba Sokoto,* as the case may be, emphasising their towns/communities (Kano, Sokoto), instead of an ethno-linguistic grouping. Indeed, even to this day, we find people adopting the names of their communities as their surnames. When the demands of modern bureaucracy and the insistence of colonial administrators compelled people to have surnames, several people simply surnamed themselves Kano, Sokoto, Shagari, Jos, etc.—indicating both an immediate clan affiliation and a less specific affiliation based on the community.[2]

In the south-west of the country, where the Yoruba are in the majority, the term "Yoruba" is used as a classificatory label for a wide range of clans and communities who describe themselves variously as Ondo, Ekiti, Oyo, Ikare, Ijebu, and so on. We should recall that the word "Yoruba" itself was originally only used to describe the people of Oyo who, before the arrival of the British, had forged an empire from a variety of diverse ethnic groups. With the arrival of the missionaries and the British colonial power, Oyo Yoruba was standardised and made available as the officially accepted variety. The development of orthography and the translation of the Bible into Oyo Yoruba served to reinforce the idea of an "original version" of the language of which other varieties are merely "dialects". Bishop Samuel Ajayi Crowther's translations of the Bible were most helpful to the proselytsing efforts of the missionaries, and made available to the first literate local *elite* a common language to which, in spite of local differences in speech and dialect patterns, they could claim allegiance. The demands of status and power meant that previously warring groups could subsume their differences and stake a common claim to an identity based on a language which had been arbitrarily chosen and imposed.

At this point we must note that geographical contiguity did play a role in all of these developments. We would not be able to otherwise explain the exclusion of Itsekiri, which shares several structural and lexical similarities with Yoruba, from this ethnic identity. In terms of linguistic affinity, Itsekiri is perhaps closer to Yoruba than some of the dialect groups which come under that label. It is possible to argue that other identity-generating factors such as myths of common origin may also have been at work here, but then again, those myths, as we well know, are necessary fictions constructed by power groups for ideological purposes. In predominantly oral societies such as these, the promotion of group solidarity often takes precedence over historical accuracy. So geographical location is a plausible reason for the exclusion of the Itsekiri, which ordinary Yoruba language speakers recognise as a sister *language* rather than as a dialect of Yoruba which it could just as well have been.

The point being made here is that language-based ethnic identities are *constructs* which arise from specific historical circumstances and ideological imperatives. Without having being socialised into standard Yoruba, it is easier for an Ikale (a dialect of Yoruba) to understand an Itsekiri (a different language) than to understand Oyo Yoruba. Examples of this kind also abound among the other majority languages. Among the Igbo, for instance, it is easier for an Onitsha to understand Ekwere (a language spoken in Rivers State), than to understand another Igbo speaker from, say, Abakaliki. The Ika people across the west of the river Niger from Onitsha, who also speak a language broadly similar to Igbo, also insist on a different ethnic identity.

These cases represent instances of the maintenance of local identities and a refusal to be placed under an imposed label. They appear peculiar merely because these "invented" ethnicities, which can serve only as descriptive categories and contrasting labels, have over time become essentialised to such an extent, that they now conceal the historical processes which led to their emergence. They have assumed the status of "authentic" essences, which are only now and again deconstructed when local identities, for whatever reasons, rise in resistance against them.

Constitutionally Nigeria is a federation, and even though years of unitary military rule have subverted the federal idea, the political and administrative structure of the country still pays lip service to the concept of federalism. There are states and state administrators or governors who are supposed to administer the country along federal lines. In the 1950s and 1960s, when there were only three regions dominated by the major ethnic groups, various minority groups rose up in protest against their marginalisation. During the ensuing civil war, the federal government broke up the three regions into twelve states, to gain the support of minorities and to allay their fears of continual marginalisation. Since then, a Pandora's box has been opened. Local identities, even within the old Yoruba, Igbo, Hausa hegemonic trinity, have staged a resounding resurgence, clamouring for new states to be created to match their own local sense of themselves as different and distinct peoples. Nigeria now has 39 states, and the clamour for the creation of still more states has not abated.

With over 400 languages available for such claiming, the absurdity of language-based identity becomes increasingly obvious. Ancient animosities, recently concealed by the newly constructed and superimposed labels of ethnic identity, have resurfaced to fracture the imposed hegemonies of the past. In Igboland, for instance, the old Anambra state was split into Enugu and Anambra states, and since then intense rivalries have developed between the two new states—sometimes degenerating to xenophobic levels. In the new Enugu state, indigenes of Anambra state are considered "outsiders" who are routinely retrenched from jobs in the state bureaucracy, to force them to relocate to their "homeland".

"African 'colonies' were really administrative fictions with nothing holding them together but the bureaucratic imagination and territorial appetite of the colonizers" (Lindfors, 1997:122). So too, ethnic identities in Nigeria were fictions constructed to fit "a language of the imagination" of particular powerful interest groups intent upon furthering specific goals or ideologies.

The politicisation of ethnicity

Apart from glossing over "dialect" and difference, the labelling of groups and the nature of the power relations between those labelled and the naming agencies, led to a tendency for the labelled group to appropriate and internalise its new identity (Erickson, 1993). According to Jenkins (1994:206): "The individual's experience of the consequences of being categorised may over time lead to an adjustment of his or her own image in the direction of the ... public image." In spite of the evidence of the resurgence of local identities in the state-creation drama in Nigeria, there can be little doubt that the major ethnic groups still command an irreducable appeal which possesses great mobilisation power in times of political crisis. The recently annulled elections in Nigeria and the re-emergence of an exclusionist Yoruba political organisation to promote the political interests of the group, show that these ethnic identities are not about to disappear. Indeed the entire tenor of public discourse points to a re-privileging of these identities.

Perhaps the real problem does not have to do with the accuracy or otherwise of these semantic labels. The problem is the internalisation and politicisation of ethnicity to the degree that it engenders conflict and, through its coercive power, forecloses other avenues through which a stake to multiple and plural identities can be made. Even though these ethnicities have no guarantees in language as they claim, they still possess such immense sentimental and symbolic power that their call acts as rallying points in periods of crisis and conflict. Their power and potency remain precisely because they have been appropriated and internalised by those so labelled. In short, they have become instruments of cultural ideology, inextricably implicated in the material and semiotic processes of culture, determining relationships, policing boundaries, and subtly maintaining the political and socio-economic mechanisms which set them in place in the first instance.

The example of an Igbo-speaking politician from the Eastern region of Nigeria reveals some of the absurdities that often arise from the ethno-linguistic classification of people. Dr Mnamdi Azikiwe, first president of Nigeria and leader of the National Council for Nigeria and the Camerouns (NCNC), thought that his party and a host of smaller affiliate groups had won an election in Western Nigeria in the 1950s. An Igbo in a predominantly Yoruba-speaking territory, he turned up in the regional parliament after the elections, expecting to take his place as premier of the region. What he had not reckoned with, was that the Action Group (AG), the opposing political party, led by a Yoruba, had deployed the bogey of ethnic identity and negotiated an alliance with the smaller parties to form a government in the region. Distraught at the turn of events, Azikwe migrated eastwards to his "homeland" across the river Niger, to take the premiership from a non-Igbo-speaking leader of his party which had won the elections in the east. The political reality of ethnic "boxing" was asserting itself, both in the events in the west, and those in the east.

Nnamdi Azikiwe, however, did not stop trying to negotiate a multiple identity for himself all his life. Born at Zungeru in the North, and having spent most of his years in Lagos in the west, he was fluent in all three major languages. But the ethnic boxes proved highly exclusionist and resistant to "outsiders". At the height of the Nigerian Civil War, when it had become fairly obvious that the Republic of Biafra (the seceding eastern region) would not survive, Nnamdi Azikiwe declared that the Onitsha people really came from Benin, and were thus also descended from the Edos. A wave of public outcry from the Igbos greeted this declaration. Azikiwe was accused of being a sell-out, a traitor and enemy of the Igbos and the Igbo cause. And once again, his effort to lay claim to another identity outside the ethnicity into which he had been boxed, was denied.

The Azikiwe story—which reads like a comedy of errors—highlights the "lighter" side of the consequences of the politicisation of ethnicity and the hermeticism of ethno-linguistic groups one labelled. The more tragic stories appear daily in the media, from the former Yugoslavia, to Rwanda and Burundi. These narratives provide evidence of the absurd depths to which we can descend once we uncritically appropriate and internalise these labels of identity.

Minorities and minority languages

There are several definitional problems associated with the use of the term "minority language" (see for example Adegbija, 1997, for a useful summary of these). Suffice it to say here that minority language, in the context of this discussion, refers to all the languages used in Nigeria— aside from the three constitutionally designated "major" languages.

In the delta region of Nigeria, where a lot of minority language groups often live in uneasy co-habitation, a local English-based pidgin has developed for purposes of inter-ethnic communication and commerce. This pidgin is particularly well developed in the Delta and River states, where there is a diverse array of ethnic groups and languages without any asserting overwhelming dominance. In the Cross River and Akwa Ibom states, where Efik and Ibibio are predominant, the language does not appear to flourish as significantly as in the former states. Nigerian pidgin is a *contact* language which allows interaction between various ethnic groups. It has no "native speakers" and therefore does not come with the cultural baggage of the other ethnic languages. The fact that Efik and Ibibio share great similarities in terms of structure, grammar and a great many lexical items, means that the minorities in the areas in which they are spoken, can reasonably do without a pidgin. The question again arises as to why they are classified as different languages, rather than as dialects of the same language.

We must remember that "the process of pidginization probably requires a situation that involves at least three languages, one of which is 'dominant' over the others" (Wardhaugh, 1986:57). In the delta region, several local languages co-exist, and the official "dominance" of English led to the development of this English-based pidgin. Pidgin would have provided access to an identity not based on ethnicity, but the common view is that pidgin is "bad" or "rotten" English and it is thus denigrated. Because it developed from the fairly uneducated lower classes, it is regarded as deficient and somewhat inferior to the "standard" languages from which it borrows. These are probably the reasons why it has hardly had any institutional backing over the years. Perhaps pidgin may some day develop into a proper *creole*. The proportion of inter-ethnic marriages in which one partner does not understand the language of the other, is increasing, and the children born out of such unions may turn out to become native speakers of a new *creole*. If and when this happens, the possibility of laying claim to an identity based on language but not on ethnicity, would have considerably improved.

Concluding remarks

In the main this chapter has attempted to examine the complex issues surrounding the question of language and identity in Nigeria. An exploration of the role of ethnicity as a complicating factor to this equation, has also highlighted the manner in which powerful interest groups have defined these ethnic identities and ensured that the "boxes" of identities remain hermetically sealed.

I conclude that despite the spurious claims of ethno-linguistic identities, they remain powerful and compelling, for they are always instrumental in attempting to block the emergence of other identities and to stifle the very possibility of their formation.

Notes

[1] I owe these insights to Dr Ibrahim Abdullah of the Department of History, University of the Western Cape, South Africa, whose in-depth knowledge of these issues further clarified my perspective.

[2] I use these terms in the sense in which Edward Said uses them in *The world, the text, and the critic* (Cambridge, Mass: Harvard University Press, 1983).

References

Adegbija, E. 1997. The identity, survival and promotion of minority languages in Nigeria. *The International Journal of the Sociology of Language*, vol. 125:5-27.

Erickson, F. & Schultz, J. 1983. *The counsellor as gatekeeper*. New York: Academic Press.

Erickson, T.H. 1993. *Ethnicity and nationalism: Anthropological perspectives*. London: Pluto Press.

Even-Zohar, I. 1985. Language conflict and national identity. Alpher, J. (ed.). *Nationalism and modernity: A mediterranean perspective*. New York: Praeger, pp. 126-123.

Hall, S. 1992. New ethnicities. In: Donald, J. & Rattansi, A. (eds). *Race, writing and difference*. London: Sage, pp. 252-259.

Harries, P. 1994. *Work, culture and identity. Migrant laborers in Mozambique and South Africa, c. 1860-1910*. London: James Currey.

Herbert, R. (ed.). 1992. Introduction. In: *Language and society in Africa. The theory and practice of sociolinguistics*. Witwatersrand: Witwatersrand University Press, pp. 1-19.

Jenkins, R. 1994. Rethinking ethnicity: Identity, categorisation and power. In: *Ethnic and Racial Studies,* 17(2):198-223.

Lacan, J. (Transl. Alan Sheridan), 1997. *Ecritis: A selection*. London: Tavistock.

LePage, R. & Tabouret-Keller, A. 1985. *Acts of identity*. Cambridge: Cambridge University Press.

Lindfors, B. 1997. *African textualities, texts, pre-texts and contexts of African literature*. Trenton, New Jersey: Africa World Press.

Louw, J.A. 1983. The development of Xhosa and Zulu as languages. In: Fodor, I. & Hagege, C. (eds). *Language Reform: History and Future 11*, pp. 371-392. Hamburg: Buske Verlag.

Maake, N.P. 1994. Dismantling the tower of Babel. In search of a new language policy for a post-apartheid South Africa. In: Fardon, R. & Furniss, G. *African languages, development and the state*. London: Routledge, pp. 111-122.

Makoni, S.B. 1996. Language and identities in Southern Africa. In: Vaughan, K. *et al.* (eds). *Ethnicity, roots meanings and implications*. Edinburgh: Centre for African Studies, University of Edinburgh, pp. 261-274.

Said, E. 1983. *The world, the text, and the critic*. Cambridge, Massachusetts: Harvard University Press.

Wardhaugh, R. 1986. *An introduction to sociolinguistics*. Cambridge, Massachusetts: Basil Blackwell.

Chapter 3

Exiting from the Existing State in Nigeria

Eghosa E. Osaghae

Introduction

Recent literature on politics in Africa and the Third World is replete with accounts of the rise of "mostly anti-system, mostly grassroots, movements with a variety of political, social and economic goals ... which are often beyond the control of the state..."[1] (Haynes, 1997:vii, 3). Another account refers to groups which interact with the state "by bypassing it ... by defining [themselves] in relation to economic, political or cultural systems which transcend the state, by submerging the state with its spectacular claims and mobilisations" (Bayart, 1991:60; Bayat, 1997).

The phenomenon described in these accounts is referred to in the literature as *exit/exiting*, defined as disengagement or retreat from the state by disaffected segments of the citizenry—into alternative and parallel social, cultural, economic and political systems which are constructed in civil society and compete with those of the state (Azarya, 1988, 1994; Azarya & Chazan, 1987; Bratton, 1989; Young, 1994).[2] This is a deviation from the *"marriage"* between citizens and the state which is consummated in terms of reciprocal rights and duties. *Exit* is commonly regarded as a strategy for coping with "a domineering yet ineffective state" (Du Toit, 1995:31), but it also represents the resistance of weak and marginalised segments which in extreme cases can lead to separatist agitation or even secession. An analytical distinction can accordingly be made between *exit from the polity* and *exit from the state*.[3]

The former involves bypassing or avoiding the organised civil order without necessarily disconnecting from the state. Such a qualified exit—which is more prevalent amongst ordinary people, for whom *exiting* is a matter of survival—results from the fact that however much they try to avoid the state, those organising the parallel systems continually need the state in some way or another. Following the example of the "Black Market" in Ghana, where two-thirds of the annual cocoa export in the early 1980s was done illegally, it has been observed that parallel systems operate with some measure of collusion from state officials (Du Toit, 1995:12). Also, voluntary ethnic and kinship self-help associations, which have historically formed the bulk of exit sites in most parts of Africa, have been the targets of the state's neo-patrimonialist designs (as has been the experience of *Harambee* in Kenya), or have themselves been involved in the nepotist and corrupt competition for state resources and patronage.

On the other hand, *exit* from the state itself is more manifestly political and *elite*-driven, and involves a high degree of, or aims ultimately at disconnection from the state. This can take the form of emigration (or exile) which has increased with the intensification of globalisation and is, *inter alia*, occasioned by the advent of so-called global citizenship, renunciation of citizenship and, at the level of the group, separatism and secession. But whether from the state or polity, *exit* amounts to a disclaimer of the state which proceeds simultaneously with a claim to ownership of the parallel sites of solidarity and self-governance. This resonates in the cultivation and adoption of counterstate identities, notably ethnic, religious and deviant antisystem identities (such as secret cult identities created by students in tertiary institutions in Nigeria). *Exit* therefore, entails movement *away from* rather than *toward* the state—a transfer of identity, loyalty and support from the state—to parallel sites in civil society, by aggrieved, alienated or marginalised citizens and groups.

This chapter is about *exit* from the state in Nigeria, which reached a crescendo in the 1980s and 1990s, with the massive emigrations of citizens abroad and an upsurge in the number, activities and significance of parallel and self-governing economic, socio-cultural and juridical systems. In the face of the increased inability of the state to provide expected public goods and services, and the authoritarian assault of personal military dictatorships which further alienated the citizenry, most ordinary people turned to various parallel identity sites—fundamentalist religious movements, ethnic self-help unions, Black Market networks, the streets, secret cults, exile, etc. for survival, refuge, reproduction and empowerment. The high profile of "shadow" state activities[4] performed by social movements and voluntary self-help organisations in areas that traditionally belong to the state, such as provision of potable water and electricity, maintenance of public schools, and security of life and property, tell the story of *exit* from the state.

But this is only the more obvious part of the story. Why, in the first place, is there such large-scale *exit*? What forms does *exit* take, and what are the parallel systems and identity sites that have developed? What identities have flowed from these sites, and how are they constructed and sustained? Is *exit* a recent phenomenon? If not, what changes have taken place over the years to incur it? Why, for example, has emigration abroad or exile become a popular form of *exit* in the recent past? How has the state responded to *exit* and its attendant withdrawal of support, which has further compounded the chronic crises of legitimacy and national cohesion it has suffered since inception? What are the implications of *exit* for Nigerian nationalism? Answers to these and other questions will be sought by first examining the factors that predispose and shape *exit*, as presented in different theoretical formulations. After this more general and comparative African discussion, the more empirical dimensions of *exit* in Nigeria will be analysed.

Exiting from the state: Theoretical perspectives

The various explanations for *exiting* can be summarised into three complementary "theories" of *exit* which explain *why* people exit from the state; *how* they exit, i.e. whether as individuals or groups, and *which categories* of people are the more likely to exit. These then are the *theory of indigeneity,* the *theory of marginalisation,* and the *theory of extraneity*, or *globalisation.*

The *theory of indigeneity* attributes *exit* to the resilience of indigenous African norms of social organisation, namely the norms of (organic) group solidarity and mutual self-help which are expressed in the practices of sharing and community—as opposed to individual—welfare. Although these norms are often presented as "naturally" African, historical evidence suggests that they evolved and became significant following the failure of pristine states to protect the interests of ordinary people in the pre-colonial era and to defend them in times of adversity. The case of "kinship", which has remained a key organising principle of *exit* structures, illustrates this historical fact. According to Ekeh (1990, 1995), kinship bonds rose to prominence in the era of the slave trade when pre-colonial states, many of them slaving states, were unable to protect their citizens from the ravages of slave raids and the dehumanising trade it fuelled—where many states in fact sold their very people into slavery! Disowned and spurned by states expected to protect them, the people were forced to rely on the (self) defence offered by parallel kinship solidarity networks which they organised to fill the void created by pristine states. The failures of the colonial and post-colonial states in crucial areas of citizen welfare and protection and, in particular, the violence and terrorism which underlay their operations, reinforced the need for kinship-based self-help networks and structures in the contemporary era.

These networks have taken on various forms—hometown associations, ethnic solidarity movements, cultural organisations, community development associations, credit societies, burial societies, etc. They have been mainly engaged in shadow state activities through self-help efforts, although governments have also been lobbied towards these ends. The main beneficiaries of these activities were, and continue to be, the home towns and ethnic home areas of the unions, but in a number of cases where patterns of residence made for ethnic concentration (such as the *sabon gari*s or "stranger quarters" in northern cities in Nigeria) and/or where strangers suffered structural discrimination, the cities of domicile also benefited (Osaghae, 1994).

Social change and modernisation have, however, brought about immense diversity in the organisation of parallel structures beyond kinship and natural affinities. Networks of self-help, community welfare, solidarity and sharing have subsequently been organised around youth interests, religion, labour, gender, professions, the community, and their like. These networks are particularly active in the informal economic sector where they have given rise to credit unions, cooperatives, and savings and loans associations. One point that emerges from all this is that *exit* is not an "anomaly" from the perspective of African social structure. It is in fact positive. The other point though, is that it is those who are excluded from state power and denied the resources, privileges and protection that flow from it, that are most likely to seek the comfort and defence provided by parallel structures.

This complements the explanation offered by the second theory, which hinges on *marginalisation*. The premise of this theory is that *exit*, like voice and loyalty, is a product of the relations of, and state power that exist amongst, the various groups or categories of people in a polity (Ake, 1985). Consequently, individuals and groups who are weak, oppressed, deprived, dominated, excluded, alienated, systematically discriminated against, and unable to influence the course of state action, in short, the marginalised, are the most likely to withdraw into parallel systems beyond the control of the state, and which offer alternative access to social reproduction, empowerment, self-worth, security, and defence against the ineffectiveness of the state. Conversely, those who wield or control state power or are its beneficiaries are the least likely to exit, but are likely to exit and confront the state when displaced from power.

The question then arises, why would marginalised groups opt for *exit* rather than confronting or challenging the state to seek redress? One answer is that *exit* is a form of protest which inherently calls for redress. The other, more practical reason, lies in the authoritarian and terrorist character of the state—hallmarked by repression, intolerance of dissenting views and opposition, as well as scant regard for constitutional rule, human rights, accountability, consultation, and responsiveness in public policy. The entrenchment of these forms of state irresponsibility and discrimination, breeds cynicism and alienation of the marginalised, who then gradually lose the sense of ownership and participation necessary to make them engage with and influence the state in a meaningful way. As the state is perceived to belong to "others", the need is felt to create "our" own "state" (read as "space"). This is the *logic of exit.*[5]

The third theory, that of *extraneity*, sees *exit* as the product of a constellation of global factors. The point of departure here is the view popularised by dependency and world system theorists, that by the very nature of their inequitable integration into the global (capitalist) system, African countries have been at the receiving end of global forces elicited and formalised in the metropole. Accordingly, aspects or forms of *exit* may be explained as part of the "susceptibility to global forces and trends" (as in the diffusion effect) or as responses to external impulses and conditions which enable local formations. One of the most established strands of the theory of extraneity, attributes the patterns of state-society relations in general to the enduring effects of colonialism. Specifically, the fact that the colonial state was an imposition whose *raison d'etre* was at variance with the interests of the colonised, who were thereby alienated, has been identified as one of the historical antecedents of *exit* from the post-colonial state, as it incurred and provoked the problem of "ownership" (Osaghae, 1998a). This strand of the theory has been criticised on the grounds that the colonial state was not a wholly colonial creation and that, even if this were the case, the post-colonial state has been reappropriated by Africans in significant ways (Bayart, 1991). The critique is valid to some extent, but it does not detract from the primacy of colonialism in understanding post-colonial formations (Ekeh, 1975). Admittedly colonialism was not only a one-way traffic, in that it was not a simple process of osmosis between coloniser and colonised, but its effects were not cancelled by the granting of political independence; so that in significant ways, the pathologies of the post-colonial state are a legacy of its colonial precursor. Institutional structures and the game-rules whereby they operate, even if now staffed by local people, carried the legacy "indirectly".

The other strand of extraneity firstly analyses *exit* as an *instance or local variant of current global trends*, and, secondly, as the *consequence* of certain global factors which encourage and facilitate *exit*. In terms of trends, studies in different parts of the world, including the advanced industrialised countries suggest that large segments of mostly marginalised groups are exiting from the state. This is attributed not only to the growing incapacity of states to satisfy the material and welfare aspirations of citizens, but also the failure of the state to respond to the demands for inclusivity, différence, and social and political democracy, which have exploded all over the world with the rise of gender, labour, and youth movements, and the ascendancy of issues of human rights and equality. People have not only retreated from the state into criminal gangs, drug networks, parallel economies, and so on, but there has also been a phenomenal increase in emigration which has given rise to the concept of "global citizenship". The popularity of "brain-drain" and "exile" as *exit* forms should be seen and analysed in this context.

The effect of globalisation is more directly apparent when we consider the conducive and facilitating roles of global factors for various forms of *exit*. Parallel economic systems—black markets, smuggling rings, piracy and trade in pirated and fake goods, and scam syndicates—cannot thrive without the collusion of international syndicates and networks which produce and purchase the goods. Drug, pornographic, criminal and prostitution networks also owe a lot to supplies and patronage from abroad, while the spread of popular music such as rap and reggae, fashion trends, and religious movements, have been supportive of the cultivation of new, mostly "deviant" identities by youth and other group categories. For example, the rise of fundamentalist Moslem sects in Nigeria has been aided by generous external support, including the awards of scholarships to students.

Furthermore, the activities and support of various transnational non-governmental organisations, as well as the World Bank, IMF and other members of the international donor community, which have ditched the pathological state in favour of civil society as the engine-room of development, have been crucial to the phenomenal increase of NGOs and other "shadow" state activities in Africa. The political forms of *exit* which involve minorities and other marginalised groups demanding local political autonomy and the right of self-determination, have been boosted by the rise of international human rights organisations and the oversight functions performed by the United Nations, European Union, Commonwealth and other international organisations, which have become more interventionist in the domestic affairs of African countries—ostensibly in furtherance of good governance and democratisation. Finally, the revolution in information technology that has produced electronic mail, cable satellite systems and the internet, has further opened up the society in Africa to global trends and forces.

Although "globalisation" is crucial to analysis of *exit* in these terms, the temptation to assume that Africans are passively or uncritically receptive to the impulses it generates, or that domestic forces do not also shape those of globalisation, should be resisted, which is the point made in Bayart's critique of the *theory of extraneity*. For example, *exit* constituencies constructed around gay and lesbian identities in Western society have not been openly embraced in most parts of Africa, because of cultural and social taboos. *Exit* therefore needs to be analysed within the context of the realities of the African situation, as resulting from a combination of *both* domestic *and* global forces. For this reason, *the theory of extraneity should be considered alongside those of indigeneity and marginalisation,* which emphasise domestic factors. It is in this sense that, as was indicated at the beginning of this section, the three theories are *complementary*.

Having attempted to explain *why* citizens exit from the state, we now turn to the more empirical aspects of this phenomenon: the particular forms and character of exit from the state in Nigeria.

Exiting from the state: Forms and character

To situate analysis of the various forms of *exit* in proper context, we shall begin with a brief outline of the empirical *state of exit* in Nigeria. From what has been said so far, it is clear that *exit* has characterised relations between the state and important segments of the citizenry for a considerable period of time, but the 1980s and 1990s were remarkable for unprecedented levels and dramatic forms of massive retreat from the state. The construction of parallel economic systems, proliferation of ethnic and kinship organisations and scores of grassroot non-governmental organisations, expansion of the scope of "self-help" shadow state functions performed by these groups, the rise of secret cults and other deviant networks in institutions of higher learning, as well as of religious fundamentalism, and the phenomenal emigration of Nigerians abroad as exiles—all attest to heightened *levels of exit*. Based on the theoretical insights provided earlier, this can be attributed to the following empirical factors.

(i) The *rapid economic decline* in the country, coupled with foreign debt and the demands of "structural adjustment", which further emasculated the capacity of the state to provide jobs, subsidise education and health care, maintain social services, protect lives and property, and even payment of salaries to civil servants. This forced people to devise various coping strategies to fend for themselves by any means, fair and foul. Some of the more popular coping strategies, especially for the ordinary people and the *lumpenproletariat*, involved *exit* from the state.

(ii) The unprecedented *levels of violent repression* and personal dictatorship unleashed by the unpopular military governments of the period. Extant and potential sites of opposition and counter-hegemony (independent media, grassroots organisations, labour unions, ethnic minority organisations, student organisations, professional associations, opposition parties, human rights and pro-democracy groups) were outlawed and suppressed, while political activists and opponents were harassed, detained, and assassinated. The execution of Ken Saro-Wiwa and other Ogoni minority rights activists, the assassinations of Dele Giwa, a popular journalist, Alfred Rewane, an old democrat, and Kudirat Abiola, wife of the late Bashorun Moshood Abiola, winner of the annulled 1993 presidential election, and the large numbers of political detainees and prisoners, were some of the "highlights" of the reign of terror which, in defiance of condemnation and sanctions by the international community, decimated non-state political space, and effectively *destroyed the social basis of democracy* in Nigeria. The reign of terror drove many people into the safety of exile. It also drastically curtailed the vibrant culture of protest and resistance for which critical segments of civil society, notably the press, popular musicians and university students, were becoming well known, thereby making criticism or confrontation with the state a less likely or attractive option.

(iii) The *capture of state power* by regional and religious hegemonies and the *marginalisation and virtual exclusion of others*, notably southerners, ethnic minorities and non-muslims from enjoying the benefits of belonging to the state. The annulment of the 1993 presidential election, which was won by the late Bashorun Abiola, a Yoruba-southerner, was believed to be the culmination of a grand design by a powerful northern cabal to keep southerners out of power.

(iv) The high degree of *insensitivity to the sufferings of the masses of the people*, as well as a *lack of responsiveness and accountability* by successive military governments in their dealings with citizens during the period. These nurtured a culture of cynicism on the part of most ordinary people and organisations, which was conducive to the stepping up of *exit* structures.

(v) The *corruption and virtual collapse of governmental structures and agencies* which further worsened the crisis of legitimacy afflicting the state. The police have been unable to keep pace with the explosive levels of violent crimes, due partly to poor funding and partly to the corruption in the force itself; the impartiality of the judiciary has been called to question because of pervasive corruption; public utility boards, including oil refineries, which are unable to provide amenities and services even with the phenomenal increases in costs which have taken them beyond the reach of most ordinary people; and a civil service that has been ruined by all forms of corruption. The worsening crisis of confidence and credibility provoked by the decay of public institutions has encouraged and accelerated the construction of parallel economic, socio-cultural and political systems. In particular, it has fed the rise of pseudo-criminal networks, syndicates and gangs of smugglers, drug dealers, and the like.

We now turn to the *forms of exit*. The various forms of exit may be distinguished on the basis of *the extent to which they approximate complete disconnection from the state* (call this *degrees of exit*) or, in more qualitative terms, according to the *character of exit* which relates to the original impetus for that option. The latter approach is adopted here, *degrees of exit* having earlier been discussed in terms of the distinction between *exit from the polity* and *exit from the state*. Following the qualitative criterion, the *forms of exit* in Nigeria can be analysed according to the following sectoral categories:

Political exit

This involves the *construction of parallel political structures*—typically autonomous political organisations (not including political parties), and aspirant local and state units within the federation, seeking varying degrees of autonomy from the state for reasons of disaffection with extant political structuration and power relations. Political exit, which often entails an element of confrontation with the state and the construction of parallel political and juridical systems, can take on a wide variety of forms. The most extreme of these include *demands for or assertion of local political autonomy, separatist agitation* or *secessionist movement*, all of which directly challenge the state and invite counter-mobilisation. The unsuccessful attempt by the Igbo-led Biafra Republic to secede from the Nigerian federation, which led to civil war (1967-70); the declaration of a Niger Delta Republic by Adaka Boro and other aggrieved youths of the Niger Delta minorities in 1967; the loud demands in the 1980s for an abrogation of the federal system and its replacement with a confederal system, by disaffected southern, especially Yoruba politicians; the threats of secession by aggrieved majority ethnic groups including, most recently, those by some Yoruba leaders to secede as Oduduwa Republic, on account of northern domination; and the separatist agitations and assertion of local political autonomy by oil-bearing minorities of the Niger Delta and other minority groups—all exemplify this extreme form of *exit*.

These forms of political *exit* are also exemplified through the politico-religious Muslim fundamentalist sects and movements, notably the Maitatsine, Izala, Shi'ite and, to some extent, the Muslim Students Society, which have since the early 1980s operated in various parts of the north of the country especially, to oppose the secularity of the Nigerian state and to demand the establishment of an Ayattolah (Iranian)-type Islamic state. Members of these movements have disconnected from the state and are governed by their own strict code of *sharia law* (parallel juridical system); refuse to subject themselves to the (supposedly unjust and illegal) authority of the secular state or to pay taxes (parallel political system); and attack adherents of other faiths who they believe must be conquered, *jihad* style, in order that their desired Islamic state be established.

Parallel to these manifestations of political *exit*, would be the *assertion of cultural, linguistic and political rights and identities*, often involving a drive for self-determination and self-governance, by weak, marginalised, excluded and dominated groups, typically minorities. Milder forms of political exit include *civil disobedience, refusal to vote in elections* (such as the decision by the Ogonis to boycott the 1993 presidential election) *or to pay taxes*, and the *symbolic assertion of the autonomy of parallel political structures* through the adoption of (alternative) "national" flags and anthems and the *resuscitation of traditional political institutions.* The declaration and celebration of "national days (and weeks)", by pan-ethnic organisations in several parts of the country, especially the Yoruba southwest, in the 1980s and 1990s, were auspicious for the articulation of such *symbolic political exit,* in this case by *retribalisation.*

The activities of a typical "national" day or week, which is presided over by the traditional leader of the ethnic group, and during which ethnic national flags are hoisted and anthems sung, include the adoption of a development plan for the next year or longer, and cultural activities and rituals which reinforce a group's identity, solidarity and autonomy. An interesting variant of *exit by retribalisation* is to be found in the emergence of what elsewhere I have called *migrant ethnic empires,* this involves the construction of "tribal authorities" headed by elected "kings", by Igbos and Yorubas in most cities in the north of the country. These "empires" perform a host of important parallel political, social, economic and judicial functions, ranging from traditional "shadow state" functions to cultural revivalism, political representation and mediation of disputes (Osaghae, 1994, 1998b).

Socio-economic exit

This is by far the most popular form of exit for most ordinary people (the urban poor, youth, students, women, unemployed, rural dwellers, the disabled or handicapped, street children)—who feel alienated, neglected, marginalised, and unprotected, and have a basic distrust of the ability of the state to redeem them. Most of these people consequently attach greater importance to the *self-help associations, networks* and *social movements* they organise and belong to, which give meaning to their lives, meet their socio-psychological needs, and perform shadow state functions which the state is unwilling and unable to perform. Many youths have turned to *ethnic and religious organisations* for solace in the face of unemployment; *women's and credit associations* have become more significant for those lacking capital to begin micro-enterprises; *traditional health care institutions* have increased in popularity as most ordinary people cannot afford the high costs of modern health care; parents who cannot afford exhorbitant fees are withdrawing their children from primary and secondary schools to Quaranic *schools and informal sector training centres* from where, on graduation, they become mechanics, traders, tailors, cobblers, carpenters, masons, drivers, etc.

The parallel structures of *socio-economic exit* can be classified into *formal* and *informal. Formal structures* which have some or other form of *institutional organisation*, include the various *ethnic associations* (hometown, village, lineage-extended family), and *pan-ethnic associations*, whose speciality is the broad spectrum of shadow state activities; *market women's associations* and *credit (esusu) societies*, which advance loans to set up enterprises for members; *farmers associations, secret cults, religious and spiritualist organisations, neighbourhood associations* such as "land-lord associations" which have virtually replaced the state in the provision of security and supply of water and electricity in their localities, and a host of *traditional associations and movements* such as age-grade societies, guilds, and women's societies. The number and variety of these organisations, especially ethnic associations, student secret cults, fundamentalist muslim sects and born-again pentecostal churches have steadily increased since the 1980s, suggesting an upsurge in the number of ordinary people retreating from the modern public sector controlled by the ailing state.

The *informal structures* on the other hand have *fleeting membership and organisation*. They mostly represent the *exit* (read as protest or resistance) of the *lumpenproletariat*: lower and under-classes, the unemployed, alienated youth, slum dwellers and the like. At one end of these structures are the *relatively autonomous informal sector constituents*—the associations and networks of street traders, hawkers, artisans, unskilled labourers, and so on— whose goal is to dominate or control the space claimed by their members and keep the authorities at bay as much as possible. There are also the *social movements* arising from religious practices such as faith healing, from popular music, such as "Fuji", "Afro-beat", and "juju", and from popular fashion which express popular *anti-system* sentiments.

At the other end of the spectrum, are *pseudo-criminal networks and gangs* of "area ('turf') boys", prostitutes, drug addicts, drug cartels, fake documents syndicates, urban street children and touts; piracy, smuggling and Black Market operators who control the illegal trade in foreign exchange—pirated goods, fake drugs, smuggled goods, and counterfeit currency. There are also the advance fee *fraud syndicates*, popularly known in Nigeria as "419", which use local and international connections, including government officials and law-enforcement officers, to dupe rich people within and outside the country. While also emphasising autonomy from the state in their day-to-day operations, the main interest of these latter networks lies in furthering the welfare of members and protecting them from the law-enforcement agents of the state.

Exile

A third form of *exit* which *straddles the political and socio-economic divide* is *exile*, or emigration abroad. This form of exile which has increased in popularity since the 1980s especially among the youth, academics and professionals, is highly *individualistic*, as the impetus for exit varies from one person to the other. Most people go into exile to escape political persecution or death by repressive governments, or for socio-economic reasons of material enhancement, better life ("greener pastures") and self-actualisation. Such exiles prefer the status of (political or economic) *refugees*, legal and illegal *immigrants* and naturalised *aliens*, to the threat to life and immiseration of remaining at home. The opportunities offered by the American *visa lottery* and *illegal visa syndicates* have further encouraged the exile traffic.

But exile is not altogether an individual matter. Exiles have formed various associations and movements abroad. Many of these resonate with, or are in fact external branches of, popular (kinship, ethnic, religious, traditional, regional, gender, alumni) associations at home, and persist in various forms of self-help development activities, some of which are targeted at constituencies back home. However, in the 1990s, with the suffocation of opposition groups at home, exile organisations underwent some form of radicalisation in response to the deteriorating political and economic conditions at home. Thus most of them, including the "traditional" ethnic and religious organisations, became outspoken critics of the government at home, demanding one form of social justice or the other on behalf of their groups.

The *radical* stage, however, belonged to the newly styled, manifestly political and sometimes revolutionary *pro-democracy* and *anti-military government movements.* Notable among the new groups are the *Association of Nigerians Abroad* which has branches all over Europe and America, *Nigerian Democratic Movement* (NDM), *National Democratic Coalition* (NADECO-Abroad), and the *National Liberation Council of Nigeria* led by Wole Soyinka. The activities of these groups have centred around exposing the atrocities of the military governments in Nigeria, mobilising the international community against them and, in concert with pro-democracy organisations at home, championing the cause of democratisation in the country. These groups have made elaborate use of information hi-tech as the *site of exit.* The internet and electronic mail have been used to stimulate debates on political issues, and to conscientise and mobilise members of the exile community against the undemocratic governments at home. These groups are also believed to have set up *Radio Kudirat,* an international opposition radio station that has been used to further the cause of the opposition movement. One interesting dimension of the political *exit* expressed in Radio Kudirat which is symbolic of the construction of a parallel political system and rejection of the state as presently constituted, is the use of the old national anthem, "Nigeria we hail thee" in place of the current anthem, "Arise O compatriots" (several student organisations within the country do the same thing when demonstrating). Another is the mobilisation and funding of non-governmental organisations within the country to oppose the state.

The other significance of exile lies in how its composition reflects the *interface of power and exit.* Where it involves large numbers of people from particular segments of the citizenry, exile becomes a good indicator of which groups suffer discrimination, marginalisation or exclusion, or whose members feel most aggrieved. The profile of those going into exile from Nigeria indicates the following:

1. Youths, academics and professionals constitute the vast majority, with women making up a significant proportion;

2. Most of the others are opposition elements—human rights and pro-democracy activists, leaders of separatist minority movements, retired military officers, fugitives and so on—who had to flee the country under threat of assassination, detention and repression;

3. Roughly 90% of all exiles come from the south of the country.

These details reveal a lot about the nature of marginalisation in Nigeria. They indicate that youths, academics and women form the bulk of the socially and economically marginalised, and that southerners are both economically and politically marginalised. With regard to the latter, it is not surprising that the activities of the opposition organisations and networks formed by political exiles, centre around southern opposition to northern domination of political power and control of the country's resources.

The response of the state

This chapter will conclude with an examination of *state response to exit* as we have analysed it. What are the implications of *exit* by important segments of the citizenry, and what dangers (or benefits) do they portend for the state? These questions need to be addressed before the response of the Nigerian state can be meaningfully analysed. Although *exit* involves retreat from the state, it *seriously challenges the state's totalising legitimacy and nation-building projects*. This is because at the core of *exit* lies a process of *denationalisation*, one that represents a weakening of the individual's loyalty to and identity with the nation-state, and a simultaneous strengthening of sites of counter-hegemonic and rival loyalties and identities. In particular, it represents the strengthening of sites of ethnic, religious and regional solidarity which are themselves claimants to rival statehood, directly challenging the state's first claim to the citizen's loyalty.

The politicisation and manipulation of these nation-challenging identities, by mostly disaffected and displaced *elites*, pose serious dangers to the survival of the Nigerian state. Being already aggrieved, it has been relatively easy for displaced and ambitious *elites* to mobilise exit constituencies against the state, thereby *transforming exit into confrontation*. Indeed, *counterstate mobilisation* has been on the increase since the 1980s.

Some of the more prominent examples include the violent eruptions of the Islamic-state seeking, fundamentalist Muslim sects (Maitatsine, Shi'ite) in various parts of the north; the uprising of the Niger Delta oil minorities, notably the Ogoni, led by the late Saro-Wiwa, and the Movement for the Survival of Ogoni people, to demand local political autonomy and adequate material compensation for the hasards of the oil industry; the rise of revolutionary opposition movements among the ranks of the exile communities abroad; and the rise of ethno-regional hegemonies and separatists, especially in the aftermath of the annulment of the June 1993 presidential election, which was regarded as the height of an alleged grand design by northern elites to exclusively control federal power.

Although resurgent *ethnicity*, *religious fundamentalism* and *regionalism* constitute the most potent threat to the state—because, as we have indicated, they involve and represent claims to rival statehood, the *effects and implications of other exit sites and identities* are equally foreboding for the state. Sites of "deviance" and pseudo-criminal networks such as secret cults on campuses, black markets, smuggling rings and underground movements, have been used for sabotage activities which represent the resistance of the oppressed, defiance, and other authority-challenging acts. For one, smugglers and foreign exchange black market operators, sometimes with the backing of powerful *elites* and state officials, sabotage official policies and regulations on trade and currency.

Area boys, touts and members of criminal gangs have been responsible for the theft of electric cable wires which cause prolonged outages of power supply, as well as the theft of other materials which paralyse public amenities and services. The phenomenal rise of violent crimes, including assassi-nations, armed robberies, and mysterious explosions of bombs all over the country, are partly attributed to elements within these *exit* sites. For example, the Edo state police command attributed the increase in armed robberies and other violent crimes in the state in the 1990s, to students of institutions of higher learning within the country, especially those who belonged to secret cults (where aspirant members of these cults are usually required to prove their loyalty through acts of bravado, which is a condition for membership, by leading or taking part in robberies, rape, drug use, or assaulting law-enforcement officers).

The wide-ranging challenges and threats posed to the state by the various forms of *exit*, cannot therefore be overemphasised. In line with its authoritarian nature and totalising agenda, one would expect the state to suppress or eliminate, where possible, the bases for these threats—indeed, the typical African state is said to be hostile to grassroots and non-governmental organisations (World Bank, 1989). But the response of the Nigerian state to *exit* in general has been more mixed. As long as the sites of exit do not constitute any apparent danger, successive governments have embraced, manipulated and even supported them, to gain political support, as we discuss shortly. This has been the lot of associations, especially ethnic associations, which operate as self-help community development associations. Even informal structures such as area boys networks have also received rehabilitation support from government. In the case of exile, the state initially pursued a patriotism campaign, urging people to remain and "salvage" the country, until the political complexion and interests of exile constituents changed.

It is when exit sites cross the threshold of tolerance and become "out of control"—that is, once they become politicised against the state or are perceived to be so—that they attract proscription, intimidation and repression. The sites of political exit, in particular the manifestly political organisations and movements, have received such treatment, while their leaders and members have been subjected to the full force of state tyranny. But even so, attempts have been made at the political and constitutional levels to address some of the underlying problems of marginalisation which give rise to political exit. The creation of more states and local government units, introduction of such consociational or power-sharing devices such as the "federal character principle", which requires that the composition of government and its agencies should be reflective of the country's federal character, and "rotational presidency", are some of the more prominent of these attempts. But they do not go far enough, and in a sense only heighten the "Father Christmas" conception of the state, which sustains neo-patronisation, because *the fundamental disjunctures between the state and society which alienates large segments of the ordinary people and causes them to disclaim it, remain unresolved.*

On the other hand, the response of the state has been more embracing of the *positive* dimensions of *exit,* especially those embodied in the shadow state activities of parallel structures which, in a sense, have helped to paper over the failings of the state and prevent what could very well have been incessant confrontation with the state by aggrieved and disaffected masses of the people. As the World Bank (1989:60) puts it: "In self-defence individuals have built up personal networks of influence rather than hold the all-powerful state accountable for its systemic failures." But the gains from these positive aspects of *exit* have not been lost on state power-holders, who have consequently capitalised on them, especially for purposes of buying political support.

Thus, self-help development activities have received various forms of support from federal and state governments. These have ranged from the encouragement given to groups to form community development associations and co-operatives, to the creation of special agencies such as the National Directorate of Employment which activated small and medium scale private enterprise, the people's and community banks which were expected to advance credit to grassroots organisations, and corporatist programmes like the Better Life (later Family Support) programme, whose goals included poverty alleviation through partnership with and funding of parallel structures. However, although they address some of the material problems that lead to *exit,* these measures do not address the more fundamental problems of distrust and lack of confidence in the ability or willingness of the state to protect the interests of ordinary peoples and their resultant disclaimer to ownership of the state. Solutions to these problems would require *changes in the character and orientation of the state,* possibly through a type of democratisation that would *make accountability, consultation and popular participation key principles of governance.* These would hopefully reduce the high incidence of *exit* attributable to the pathologies of the post-colonial state, leaving intact the *positive forms of exit* which derive from indigenous traditions of solidarity and self-help.

Notes

[1] The use of the concept of the "state" has become so loose that one often has difficulty knowing when the intended meaning is actually "government", "ruling class", "personal ruler", or "regime". While all these relate to specific aspects of the state and can actually be regarded as its embodiment, it is important to specify the meaning of the concept. In this chapter, "state" is used in its most inclusive sense.

[2] Following Albert Hirschman's famous categories, relations between these movements and civil society at large, and the state, have been characterised as *exit* or disengagement, which involves retreat into parallel economic, socio-cultural and political systems; *voice* or confrontation, which involves resistance and opposition; and *loyalty* or collaboration, which entails partnership with the state (Azarya, 1988; Lemarchand, 1992). However, these categories are not mutually exclusive and could in fact be seen as points on a graded continuum which starts at "complete withdrawal" (through secession, for example) and "opposition" at one end, to "complete acquiescence" on the other. This way, *exit* may be perceived as a variant of voice or resistance, as is clear from Scott's (1985, 1990) characterisation of peasant and underclass retreat as the resistance of the weak.

[3] I am grateful to Professor Ali Mazrui for drawing my attention to this important distinction.

[4] By "shadow state activities" is meant the production of public and social goods by parallel non-governmental organisations (NGOs). Such activities as the provision of credit and recreational facilities, building of schools, police posts, postal agencies and hospitals, construction or maintenance of roads, and award of scholarships undertaken by community development associations and other NGOs, through self-help efforts, constitute the core of shadow state activities.

[5] However, as we noted above, *exit* does not preclude confrontation with the state to seek redress; in fact, *exit* as a matter of *political expression*, is not inconsistent with "confrontation", as it also usually embodies some form of symbolic or silent protest and resistance on the part of the oppressed.

References

Ake, C. (ed.). 1985. *Political economy of Nigeria*. London & Lagos: Macmillan.

Azarya, V. & Chazan, N. 1987. Disengagement from the state in Africa: Reflections on the experience of Ghana and Guinea. *Comparative Studies in Society and History*, 29(1).

Azarya, V. 1988. Reordering state-society relations: Incorporation and disengagement. In: Rothchild, D. & Chazan, N. (eds). *The precarious balance: State and society in Africa*. Boulder: Westview Press.

Azarya, V. 1994. Civil society and disengagement in Africa. In: Harbeson, J.W. et al. (eds). *Civil society and state in Africa*. Boulder, CO & London: Lynne Rienner.

Bayart, J-F. 1986. Civil society in Africa: Reflections on the limits of power. In: Chabal, P. (ed.). *Political domination in Africa*. Cambridge: Cambridge University Press.

Bayart, J-F. 1991. Finishing with the idea of the Third World: The concept of the political trajectory. In: Manor, J. (ed.). *Rethinking Third World politics*. London & New York: Longman.

Bayat, A. 1997. Un-civil society: The politics of the "informal people". *Third World Quarterly*, 18(1).

Bratton, M. 1989. *Beyond the state: Civil society and associational life in Africa*. Boulder, C.O.: Lynne Rienner.

Du Toit, P. 1995. *State-building and democracy in Southern Africa: A comparative study of Botswana, South Africa and Zimbabwe*. Pretoria: Human Sciences Research Council.

Ekeh, P.P. 1975. Colonialism and the two publics in Africa: A theoretical statement. *Comparative Studies in Society and History*, 17(1).

Ekeh, P.P. 1990. Social anthropology and two contrasting uses of tribalism in Africa. *Comparative Studies in Society and History*, 32(4).

Ekeh, P.P. 1992. The constitution of civil society in African history and politics. In: Caron, B. et al. (eds). *Democratic transition in Africa*. Ibadan: CREDU.

Ekeh, P.P. 1995. Kinship and civil society in post-colonial Africa. (Mimeograph).

Haynes, J. 1997. *Democracy and civil society in the Third World: Politics and new social movements*. Cambridge: Polity Press.

Lemarchand, R. 1992. Uncivil states and civil societies: How illusion became reality. *Journal of Modern African Studies*, 30(2).

Osaghae, E.E. 1989. The character of the state, legitimacy crisis, and social mobilisation in Africa: An explanation of form and character. *Africa Development*, 14(2).

Osaghae, E.E. 1994. *Trends in migrant political organisations in Nigeria: The igbo in kano*. Ibadan: IFRA.

Osaghae, E.E. 1998a. Rescuing the post-colonial state in Africa: A reconceptualisation of the role of civil society. Paper presented at the International Colloquium on State and Civil Society in Africa, University of Abidjan, Cote d'Ivoire.

Osaghae, E.E. 1998b. Hometown associations as shadow states: The case of igbos and yorubas in Kano. In: Warren, M. et al. (eds). *Hometown associations: Indigenous knowledge and development in Nigeria*. London: Intermediate Technology Publications.

Scott, J. 1985. *Weapons of the weak: Everyday forms of peasant resistance*. New Haven: Yale University Press.

Scott, J. 1990. *Domination and the arts of resistance*. New Haven: Yale University Press.

World Bank. 1989. *Sub-Saharan Africa: From crisis to sustainable growth*. Washington DC: The World Bank.

Young, C. 1994. In search of civil society. In: Harbeson, J.W. et al. (eds). *Civil society and state in Africa*. Boulder: Lynne Rienner.

Chapter 4

Parallel Society in the Democratic Republic of Congo

Tshikala K. Biaya

Introduction: Parallel society as a concept

The concept of a "parallel society" poses a problem in itself, since the adjective, up to now, was only reserved for the economy, although it affects the dominated society in its entirety, and creates a new set of problems, that of a politically and economically marginalised society operating independently from state structures, while living on national territory. Furthermore, its members recognise each other as citizens of the country, but they do not abide by its laws (duties and obligations). If, in the economic context, such a phenomenon has not been observed to this day, the experience of the Congolese society—influenced by a century-long history of arbitrary state colonial and postcolonial predation, exploitation and violence—has indeed allowed such an entity, operating within complex relationships made up of insubordination and illegality and highlighted by a quest for greater democracy. The subject "parallel society" nevertheless pertains to the organised ethnic population making up the "local state", and is at the same time the result of a mode of domination and of a model of accumulation which the central State has resorted to in order to maintain itself and uphold the leadership.

In this chapter our purpose is not to study the causes or the manner in which the current crisis has emerged and delineated the different social and political constituents of Congolese society. On the contrary, the subject of our analysis remains the constituents, the operation and the meaning of such a parallel society: how did it establish itself; how does it operate to enable it to give multipolar identity to the Congolese; and what is its value in Congolese nationalism? This identity, the historicity of which rests within the framework of a regime of domination, hinges as much on the postcolonial nation, as on the ethnicity and regionalism created from the beginning of colonial times.

The analysis of a "parallel society" will not follow the simplistic dualism which, in political science and African sociology, consists of opposing practices of leaders and the *elite*—referred to as "the top"—to politically popular modes of action or the hidden resistance of the masses—referred to as "the bottom" (Bayart, 1987; Scott, 1985). On the contrary, more so than evidenced in this simple dualism, there exists a complexity in political, social, economic and cultural relationships and relations that is pervasive in global society, and that eats away at the state territories in which "the leaders" and "the led" have set up their actions and activities. This dynamic has woven a framework in which their politically conflicting relationships are, however, included. Faced with the establishment of a parallel society, the analysis of the criminalisation of the state, as expected, and as stimulating as it may be, offers few avenues for comprehending the Congolese parallel society as a politico-economic, historic and culturally autonomous entity, since its introduction into "legalism" resting on national and international "illegality", limits the analysis to criminal behaviour (Bayart, Ellis & Hibou, 1997). Since the analysis of such societies is not its subject, it takes into account neither the various dynamics that make up and transform such a society, nor the analysis of practices marginalising the central state in Congo. In its efforts and performance against the central and hegemonic state, the parallel society has benefited as much from the contribution, whether consciously or not, of the post-colonial Congolese ruling class—eager to further "tap into" the wealth—as it has from the constraints of globalisation.

Two factors have stimulated and strengthened local power that relied on the ethnic power already in place: unauthorised domination and the consequences of disastrous national policies which have, furthermore, started political opposition and contestation for the same dominating regime. This complex process can only be analysed if we accept that *illegality*, used politically, has established itself as a feature of this societal landscape—a feature from which the Congolese population has negotiated its own existence as ethnic individuals and citizens of the Republic. And, based on this feature—this foundation—they have set up strategies to fight, indeed to rally the State against the interests of the national state and international financial institutions, without withdrawing unto itself. On the contrary, they deploy a dynamic participation in the world economy from ethnic and regional economic networks developing on the world market, while adhering to local economic structures resulting therefrom. According to the ideology in place, this structure is intended for the survival of the ethnic group or of the region. We will elaborate on this later.

In this process the parallel society has an economic foundation (as minimal as it may be), which varies from one ethnic group to the other, indicating that the process of political exclusion that Ilunga-Kabongo (1984:13-28) analysed in terms of "zone of existence" and "zone of non-existence" of the "Zairian" civil society, has created an unexpected path that became more complex after 1984 (Biaya & Omasombo, 1993:97-127). The predatory practices of the ruling class not only desecrated and forced the population to live "outside" of the state, they also allowed them to innovate living conditions in which the urbanisation of villages and the metamorphosis of cities into villages, generated new social reconstruction and political configurations, thus creating a civil society in which the relationships and power games travelled from the village to Kinshasa, the capital, the place of state decisions, whether negotiated or converted into cash.

In this context of unruly modernity, establishing itself with the help of subversive practices (Biaya & Bibeau, 1998:5-13), the state has stopped invading the bush, while the bush has invaded the city with its unusual practices, its economic network, and its political ethnic culture. From that moment, the "governance" or "governmentality" of Congo takes a disconcerting direction for the ruling class, the *elite* and researchers, including the World Bank. And it is in the heart of this social and political "formality" that we will attempt to research nationalism and the meaning thereof in the Democratic Republic of Congo.

Parallel society, a revenge of political marginalisation

Political and economic marginalisation

The century of Congolese "modernity" has been a long night during which the imposition of the modern state by colonisation was an administrative despotism at a lesser cost than the state of Mobutu and its leadership. "Mobutucracy" continued until the travesty of the state, which only had international legitimacy, while the colonial and postcolonial ruling class had criminalised the State from its very inception. Three stages illustrate this establishment of the parallel society through the dual mechanism of political and economic marginalisation which, in turn, allowed citizens to flee from arbitrary state practices to manage themselves; sometimes within a context of violence where the arsonist hand of the state often served contradictory and hardly "rational interests" in political terms.

Among the various periods and syntheses of the history of the Congo, those of the national sovereign Conference of Congo given in the general report thereof (Kinkela, 1993:135-199) summarised this history as follows: "The history of the Congolese people has always been that of an ill-suppressed rebellion, exploding in regular cycles with unusual fury" (Kinkela, 1993:136). Kinkela divided the history into five stages, the fifth of which started in 1990, and is still nowhere near its end. The colonisation by Belgium succeeded in imposing an administration replacing the state, with the help of the colonial "ethnographic library" and of the army, which tamed the various rebellions and resistance against the colonial order. It started by dividing the ethnic population into tribes, granting them a forged ethnic identity, which represented the best inclusion of the subject in colonisation. The equation "no tribe, no identity", implied that the person who was made to be part of a tribe, was eligible for employment. Neither of the two colonies (the independent state of Congo and the Belgian Congo) had the Western Weberian administrative referent or the model of a colony in the usual sense. Willame describes it as follows: "This colonial State is not at all or hardly 'rational', it is not legal either. The (arbitrary) division into territories, the confirmation and/or nomination of (pseudo) chiefs, schooling, currency dealings, military recruitment and hard labour are the expression of a progressive 'administratification' of the colony, not that of political consent from the subjugated community" (Willame, 1992:213-214). The post-colonial regime which managed to oust Lumumba and the nationalists from power since 1960, by inciting civil wars that the first government could not control, including the Belgian invasion and the secessions, concealed the implementation of a dual international strategy conducted by Belgium and the United States. Belgium wanted to recover the colony it had dropped in haste but which was already coveted by the free world; the United States applied themselves in deploying African policy relying on Mobutu, while helping themselves to a rich and strategic territory for the control of Black Africa, which they had allowed the Berlin conference to seise.

This strategy culminated in the setting up of a ruling class, aware enough of its precarious situation in linking its interests to powerful western companies—as wrote J.P. Sartre in 1961. Despite the end of the cold war and the collapse of the Communist block, this logic of "interest" would only collapse in 1992 with the coming into power of Clinton, while Belgium, disillusioned and ridiculed by this neo-colonial policy, its institutions and its contradictions, withdrew from the game in 1990.

In the meantime the post-colonial state created a political system in which arbitrary conduct and uncertainties became the rule in everyday life and in the creation of a political marginalisation supported by increasing state violence. Furthermore, and in order for this violence to function "effectively", it required a security system and an army devouring enormous amounts of money as this political system—Mobutucracy—was being established through a "unitarian party" (1967), "authenticity" (1971), the "party-State" (1974), and the "cult of personality" (1980). This regime rested exclusively on the systematic plunder of resources by the ruling class (Verhaegen, 1978:374-379). The challenging of the political system, which started early in 1963 with the armed struggle of Pierre Mulele and the movement of the second independence, resumed in 1982 with the creation of UDPS and the supposed peoples' desire for a return to multipartism and federalism. In truth, it is the "therapy" to the economic crisis which the World Bank and the IMF as well as other donors, imposed, that eliminated this system, the limits of which were foreseeable. The conditionality of democratisation of the regime—as a guarantee of good economic management—turned the water canons on an opposition that would harden even if it ended up in pitiful disorganisation *vis-à-vis* the dictator. Nevertheless, it obtained the national conference in 1991, and the transition in 1992.

During that time, the structural violence of the state was growing in a manner inversely proportional to its already precarious and weak foundation. Depelchin (1991) indicates that back in 1930, investments had already dried up for this giant. The 1967-1973 economic recovery, after civil wars and rebellions (1960-1967) (Kankwenda, 1993:243-263), allowed the country to give in to superficial modernisation through the project referred to as "Objective 80"—at that time, the Congo would have become a developed country! This programme caused technological imperialism, systematic plundering of national resources and embezzlement of foreign aid, the "balance" of which is a debt of close to 14 billion dollars and the emergence of some two hundred rich families. By 1977, all the efforts this regime invested in aimed more at the upholding of Mobutu's power than at the management of the national economy, which was in a distressed and disastrous state. The IMF regretted it and the donor community bore the cost. The second republic (1965-1992), can be summarised as the absence of the state in Mobutu's Congo.

Elungu, the philosopher, could not have qualified this autocratic regime better when characterising it as being the one that dedicated its bankruptcy to three blatant "orders of disorder— the order of subversion, which bases society on the will of the arbitrary power of a person presumed absolute because he is armed; the order of corruption, which institutes private law to replace the law of labour and the law of society; and the 'order of perversion', because it rebels against everything relating to value" (quoted by Kinkela, 1993:139).

Sites and strategies of the parallel society

Beyond a daily life in *trompe-l'oeil* that unfurls in scientific literature on Congo, and beyond the inadequacies of global analysis, parallel society actually managed to establish itself from sites in which the State has always refused to be effective. It is in this interface between the "real Congo" and "national reality" in which the Congolese live, that the parallel society has positioned and established itself. It has taken *illegality as its strategic basis*, and political ethnic culture as a site to generate ethnic power. The latter, as I have described elsewhere, is a power system based on ethnic groups—a historical reality—and its accompanying political culture. "It nurses a social project and has a socio-political organisation, sometimes minimal, that manages its power niche. Such a niche is negotiated with the hegemonic central State" (Biaya, 1998a:110).

Ethnic power has enabled the planning of this society around a series of institutions and contemporary ethnic personalities, while conducting economic activities. It negotiates its existence with the regime, with which it shares the profits resulting from these economic enterprises. On the other hand, Mobutu's regime was so cunning that it cannibalised foreign aid without attacking international financial institutions up-front. It is this "margin of manoeuvre" (Biaya & Omasombo, 1993:97-127) that remained open, the more so because Mobutu had succeeded in imposing upon them a corrupt technocrat familiar with the theatrics of duplicity, so that these same institutions knew nothing about the "hot and cold" which this senior official—L. Kengo wa Dondo—was blowing to maintain his class in power until 1997. He applied double standard neo-liberalism from the redistributing state. In 1992, the IMF and World Bank reforms proved to be useless and vacuous in the face of "Zaire, a soft stomach devouring any investment", according to E. Blumenthal. When Mobutu's death became evident, this technocrat fled to the West, leaving behind a country "objectively" in abject poverty.

This analytical canvas allows for a resumption of MacGaffey's discussion (1987:345-349, 370-371) on the concept of "parallel economy". This adjective, once formalised, becomes pertinent and justified when substituting "economy" with "society" in reference to Congo-Kinshasa.

Indeed, ethnic power or the local state would take over and control entire economic sectors being developed in the "Zairian dereliction", and would benefit from the political apathy of intellectuals, the latter either concealing their anxiety and powerlessness in the face of state violence, or experiencing and/or attempting to integrate the circle of power and enrichment by 1977, since the Zairian civil society was limited to 200 rich families. Let us, at a glance, review the different economic "zones" of Congo, in order to understand this phenomenon of formation of the parallel society and its horisontal and vertical relations. Willame gives a breakdown of activities by geographic sector and by the nature of the resources available within them. The six border areas (East Province, Katanga, Kivu-South, Kivu-North, Lower Congo and the Equator) and the central area (East Kasa and West Kasa), consolidated their economy after 1985 and availed themselves of substantial autonomy *vis-à-vis* the central state. They integrated the ethnic *elite* into their midst by 1988, with committees of ethnic urban and rural associations right up to the village. They also supported the opposition to the regime in place through the event of the 1980-90 period: the birth of a popular but legally clandestine party, UDPS. Indeed, the extraordinary congress of the party-state of 1988 completed the victory of the parallel society against the Mobutu state, which made vain attempts to reform the administration and propose decentralisation as a solution to the political crisis that had developed in tandem with the economic one. Members of the congress who had come from "in-house" rejected all plans for an administrative division, or a new division of the country into tribes that would undermine the foundation of the established parallel society. The failure of this final attempt by central powers to break the parallel society, confirmed the entrenchment of ethnic power, the solidity of its cultural foundation having effected its historicity.

However, during the same period, the blossoming of the informal sector was only the tip of an economic iceberg that colonisation put in place as a reward for shaping and reinforcing the ethnic group, so that the Mobutu regime and its vote-catching, which rested on ethnic manipulation, ended up consolidated and imposing to the population. This ethnicity of the parallel society, different from political and administrative tribalism of the ruling class, is above all a historicity and an interpretation on the part of the population of their own local and national history. And it is from this thought process—sometimes erroneous—that this same population would organise and support their economic practices, thanks to ethnic ideology. Thus, adjoining the small shop such as lolema (Kisangani), small domestic cultivation (market garden produce, vegetables), adjoining the village-city of the fruit of cultivation—the barter between village inhabitants and small crafts industries developed—and an interregional trade was positioning itself, as well as international trade beyond the borders of the country and connecting to international networks (Biaya, 1985:65-84; MacGaffey, 1987). This illegal import-export trade imposed the need and necessity for its development, to guarantee itself as an ethnic protector, strong enough to negotiate the terms of its "existence" with the ruling and bourgeois class, either through business partnerships or through a payment system. Religious and political "ethnic" personalities carried out this "task" on the basis of ethnicity, which they broadened onto regionalism where needed. Thus we witnessed the undermining of the law forbidding ethnic organisations; and privatisation of mining operations, forbidden long ago, became more "flexible" or otherwise regained momentum. In return, some places of popular ethnic rebellion quietened down. This logic of neo-liberalism, while furthering the strengthening of ethnic regrouping in the amateur development of mining concessions (gold, diamond), as well as the export of agricultural products (tea, coffee, cinchona, etc.), also propelled—following the same logic—the export of mining products from cannibalised companies (spare parts, cobalt, pewter, copper, etc.); and it stimulated the emergence of carefully contrived "ethnic solidarity" towards the development of the province controlled by ethnic intellectuals. Various associations and local NGOs blossomed and set objectives to resume control of what the state had abandoned or was unable to control, such as local universities, regional development councils, and NGOs.

Without succumbing to blind admiration for the belief that the informal sector is an economic success even while it is incapable of accrual, we have to admit that this substantial newly-born bourgeoisie in some areas was able to accrue and capitalise on its assets. From that time, the dwindling "legal society"—or the central state—and the growing parallel society—became complementary in their economic and political functions at top level, where the ruling class and the ethnic bourgeoisie were sharing the profits. This "conviviality" was sufficient to secure autonomy to the parallel society. In 1995 the latter ended up managing monetary areas in which the American dollar rules; and secondly, the three currencies hit by the central powers continue to circulate in one (and not in the other) ethnic and commercial area based on a logic of fighting galloping inflation, reaching 10 000% in 1995. The annual state budget did not reach the 230 million dollars, representing one-fifth of the annual turnover of the only city of Mbujimayi reaching one billion (Biaya, 1998b). However, specialisation in illegal economy and trade—or of the parallel society—imposed itself, based on materials produced and their international trading network. The money thus earned is used for importing goods. A whole "economy of withdrawal", managed by local ethnic networks, has established itself with leading cities such as Mbujimayi, Kinshasa, Butembo, Lubumbashi, Bunia, etc. which have become platforms and places of power of the parallel society, with its local economy and civil society defending it against the decaying state, the latter reduced to an administrative role. Interregional economic links were coupled with international links, enabling better circulation of imported goods, although sometimes in disastrous transport conditions, given that roads are almost non-existent and reduced to tracks. Finally, these "economies" of parallel society are not created without bloodshed, and they operate by paying "protection" to customs officials, policemen and other officials, for its own survival and the protection of its "lords".

In opposition to what Longandjo, a development sociologist, maintained— the power of the state is not evaluated on its failure to maintain itself as "res publicae" and in managing hunger, illnesses and violence, but its marginalisation lies at the origin of the dynamism of a parallel society nurtured by its ethnicity and political culture engendered in terms of its existence, giving it popular legitimacy in the face of a gangster-state. This is symptomatic and deserves to be mentioned. When

ADFL (the Alliance of Democratic Forces and Liberation) seised Kisangani in 1997, Kabila suspended this gold and coffee "traffic"; but soon thereafter the parallel society—this socio-political burden—forced him to exercise moderation in the bureaucratic and technocratic language which was about to cause famine where it had not existed before. This struggle against "Mobutist" anti-values, in order to establish new values, was postponed until later. Whether he liked it or not, he authorised this illegal trade which he had suspended, to resume.

Multipolar identities, antagonism and interests

The question of identity or identities is the next focus of attention, since it moulds the individuals and communities making up the parallel society. As mentioned above, any identity is a construction; and as with any construction, it is subject to evolution and death. Following their particular history, the Congolese have developed a multipolar and plural identity, emergent upon colonial and postcolonial policies.

Furthermore, it is interesting to note that when Mobutu came into power, he started a jealous centralism, thus falsely displaying his support for "Lumumbist" nationalism and the will of the regime to undo tribal divisions in the country. This policy, resuming the colonial one consisting of forbidding tribal associations, did not succeed in stopping political exclusion and economic marginalisation due to predatory management. Not only did it revive colonial ethnic identities but it also established new identities, either claim makers of regional or ethnic identities, which did not contradict the national identity and Congolese nationality. Mass participation in various associations, indicates that the first identities were developed around big ethnic (or tribal) groups, and political parties from the advent of independence (1960-1965). These representations benefited from the experience of political and economic marginalisation of the second republic, as they expressed themselves in economic and commercial competition occurring in urban areas. Let us take the case of the Luba-Kasa group to illustrate a way of creation of postcolonial identities.

The post-colonial Luba identity came about by 1959, by rejecting the fabricated colonial urban identity. Instead, this group, urbanised since 1921-1945, and returning from a forced national exodus caused by the civil war for independence (1959-1960), established the city of Mbujimayi and its province, where to this effect, it claimed a Nkonga identity, namely that of "the unifier". This new identity was the fruit of the urban experience and political history which the Luba succeeded in creating in the autonomous state of South Kasa. This identity, breaking away from the colonial one following the "betrayal of the Whites", evolved rapidly in a direction distinct from that of members of the same ethnic group that had not supported the exodus or its ethnic ideology, and that stayed in colonial cities and places of ethnic persecution. Thirty years later, the colonial Katanga identity resurfaced and, organising itself on the basis of regionalism, became genocidal with the help of the central state and its ethnicity; and was marshalled against these Luba, who had remained behind in 1960 and whom it forced to return to the original Kasa abandoned three generations earlier. At the heart of this warmongering ethnicity, which is still predominant in the Great Lakes region and strongly rooted in some parts of the country, is the "tribalist" identity of the colonised—moulded by the coloniser and nurtured by postcolonial power. The warmongering ethnic identity lacks a sound and well thought-out historical foundation, because when the regional enemy disappears, it becomes fragmented and attacks the ones closest to it, who may be yesterday's ally. The example of the East province illustrates this clearly. In Kisangani, between 1982-1993, and as soon as the Bakuyakya (foreigners or Congolese born elsewhere) withdrew from the urban political game, competition for urban management (chamber of commerce, town council, municipality, etc.) rejected any applicants from persons born outside the Tshopo district or belonging to any other ethnic group of this province.

Furthermore the integrationist policy of the state and its "Authenticity" (1968-1975) (MacGaffey, 1982:49-70), which turned into exhibitionism, nonetheless succeeded in giving the Congolese a national identity, which does not exclude the ethnic, urban or rural one that the parallel society calls upon and establishes for the purposes of its own reproduction. Thus we saw the Luba intellectuals, the first wave of nationalists, defending the South-Kasa secession and turning it around into provincial autonomy in 1960-1962, although they had been turned back from this province by lesser intellectuals who had seised the pseudo-secessionist state of Kasa. During the clandestine time of the UDPS, Mobutu, evoking "ethnicism", accused this party of being "a matter for the Luba", but its architects—Luba for the most part—were more perceived as "good and true Zairians", which means "nationalists and Luba at the same time" to their fellow countrymen from other ethnic groups, which also have this plural identity. However, when it is a question of the culture of leisure, referred to as "ambiance", founded upon the trilogy of "wine, women and song" (Biaya, 1996:345-370), popular representation concurs that the Ngbandi, member of the Mobutu tribe, is immoral and perverse; the fearful, obsequious and deceitful Kongo is a good musician and a good dancer, and that the marriage of an intelligent Luba to a woman from the Equator (who steals), will produce a child with Kongo identity, etc. The multipolar aspect of identity also includes nationalism. As proof, we need only the example experienced during democratisation. In April 1991, while fights between the parallel society of Mbujimayi and the army continued for six days, over an intervention from the army to punish the owner of the bar where a meeting of UDPS took place, a tacit truce was observed by the belligerents. They all went to church on the Sunday morning, and in the afternoon, watched the football match for the African Cup between Congo and Gabon. By evening the fighting had resumed. National identity is more than a simple matter of a "passport" needed for travel, and goes hand in hand with a certain national pride that the second republic and the parallel society have evoked and inspired in the Congolese.

However, we would not share the assertion according to which ethnicity disappears in ambiguity under the impetus of urbanisation (Willame, 1992:212). On the contrary, when its multipolarity and flexibility are wrongly perceived and are not experienced by the analyst, they become the main factor of its various transformations. Above all, ethnicity bears the mark of the other player participating in its elaboration. Thus, entirely to the contrary, ethnic identity is strong and widely felt in urban areas where "polyglotty", numerous languages, inter-ethnic and cultural relations are numerous and sometimes labile—more so than in a moderately homogenous rural environment where it seldom has to compete with other ethnic identities. Besides, a person's name is the first indicator of firstly clannish individualisation, and secondly individualisation of the state, since the ethnic group of the individual is recorded in the national identity document. This reality of individual identity operates according to biographic law—says Bastide—which is enriched by our experience and accompanies us throughout our public life, starting from our private life and early childhood. In the urban Congolese context, it is as awkward as it is surprising and pleasant for a newcomer to the city—mohuta—enquiring about a wrong address—to be asked what tribe he belongs to; for as soon as he answers the question, he will, as a matter of course, be sent to consult a member of his ethnic group living in the area. However, the flexibility of identity allows for it to be changed, fractionalised, even rejected in the course of life and in the exercise of political, social and cultural dealings. The proof is there with the downfall of the Mobutu regime which, failing to ensure quick economic recovery, engenders an identity uprising resulting in the exercise of conflict implied and given in the new "unitarian" party political regime: Kabila is a conservative "Mobutist"! A tailor-made anti-democratic and anti-nationalist identity is already in place in the DRC.

Which nationalism is on the move?

This analytical description of the Congolese drama, as strange as it may be, with its weak and strong points, gives a glimpse of a will of the people to express the political thought of: "let's do something about this situation", which is the main theme of any political thought or action. "Politics are creative inventions", writes Wamba-dia-Wamba (1993:96). There is tension within the struggle which has characterised the history of the Congo for a century already. The Lumumba drama is very much like that of the Congolese people. The Congolese nationalist trend has been disrupted several times in the course of various periods, but without significant success—the messianic movement that started in 1915 on the Equator with Maria N'Koy, the rebel, Kimbangu, the catechist (1919-1921), and the female prophet Kaki (1930-1931), from the Pende, would have to wait for Lumumba for a better approach and a better knowledge of the foreign enemy: Belgian colonialism. But Lumumba would never be too anxious to capitalise on his achievements: independence and the start of a democratic and supra-tribal society; for once again, he became prisoner of his three enemies, including an old one. The Binza party was born under the leadership of Mobutu and financed by America and Belgium, whose united anti-Lumumba campaign had the support of the UN Secretary General Dag Harmaskjöld. This nationalism was expressed soon after his assassination, through civil wars and uprisings of the working class which plagued the country from 1963 to 1967. Passing through the underground forces of Mulele, to the university campus, Mobutu's pro-Western regime was eager in carrying out the students' massacre in 1969, as well as the elimination of Mulele a few months earlier, in October 1968. The Shaba wars in 1977 and 1978 brought about a new change in that the secessionists of yesterday, from Katanga, reverted to nationalism. However, the National Liberation Front of Congo (FNLC) was defeated by the massive intervention of French, Moroccan and Belgian forces and Mobutu's army, supported by American logistics.

It is also within the parallel society establishing itself that the anti-neo-colonial nationalism became a reality and resumed the struggle for new independence. Its image is no longer that of an ideology of passivity having to face the truth and miseries sweeping the country. With progressive and global prospects, from 1959 to 1992, that is for 30 years, Congolese nationalism had to face a series of rebellions of the working class: the uprising which occurred on 4 January 1959, resulting in independence; the civil wars (1960-1963); the insurgencies (1963-1967), the students' protests, the parliamentary rebellion, the workers' strikes, the self-criticism of intellectuals, the students' massacre (1969, 1971, 1989, 1990), the creation of underground movements (1976,1982), the protests and marches organised by women between 1987 and 1990 which culminated in the national sovereign conference of 1991-1992. These different stages and struggles against colonisation and the post-colonial state, were intended to achieve the creation and emancipation of a national democratic society. In this context the parallel society becomes a type of nationalism in itself—spontaneous at the start—that benefited UDPS in that it was its battle horse to usher in the national sovereign conference which saw the end of the second republic and opened the door to democratic transition (1982-1992) (Biaya, 1998b).

Despite Mobutu's departure, the AFDL, then in power, did not take into consideration the transition that resulted from the national sovereign conference. That party prolonged the transition which finally identified itself with the "day-to-day management" of power. In its ambiguous and historical sense, it failed to capitalise on the internal nationalist movement. Its undefined and unclear policies sent no signals of real control of the popular and militant nationalism that seemed to characterise its accession to power. In short, the same symptoms of a newly-born "Mobutism" are becoming apparent at regional and international levels, and those of an ageing "Mobutism" at national level.

This regime is in fact strongly inclined to negotiate its stability between a regional African policy wrongly integrated and negotiated, and an economic interest pointing towards the oblivious West, and which contradicts the anti-neo-colonial Lumumba ideology which the regime pretends to defend. Washington did express its view of the new Congolese regime in the following terms: "Kabila is not an asset but a liability". We emphasise. What responsibility? When Museveni managed to be Mobutu's successor just as Clinton replaced Bush in this era following the cold war. With the third millennium ahead, Museveni could, with great skill and intelligence, serve or cover the interests of the United States in this tormented Great Lakes region as much as Mobutu did in the past approve the anti-Communist and reactionary strategic American policy in Central and Southern Africa. On the other hand, at national level, the national parallel society and its sites remain deeply involved in the criminalisation of the state—with the help of international economic networks, coupled with the impedimenta of an ill-controlled ethnicity which reappears suddenly since it finds resources in and/or the rest of the AFDL covering the "tribalism" of revenge of the Katangese or Tutsis, which in turn rests on the logic of "amends for the wrongs of the colonial past" for the former, and "postcolonial" for the latter.

In this context there are fears that the present regime may not be as nationalist or "Lumumbist" as it pretends to be, and that in this situation of postcolonial nationalism, the conservative endogenous forces based on ethnicity may be stronger than those with new ideas. In contrast to the other identities rooted in historicity, whether genuine or erroneous, the history of Congolese nationalism has taught us a lesson, namely the weakness of nationalist identity is that it is just like a garment that can be worn or discarded, depending on the circumstances. Fortunately for nationalism that is genuine, just as for a religious order, one cannot judge a book by its cover, nor does the attire represent nationalism. It is its reflexive experience of breaking with the past, and for change in view of the democratic transformation, which constitutes the measure of that experience.

References

Bayart, J.-F. 1987. *L'Etat en Afrique*. Paris: Fayard.

Bayart, J.-F., Ellis, S. & Hibou, B. 1997. *La criminalisation de l'Etat en Afrique*. Paris: Editions Complexe.

Biaya, T.K. & Bibeau, G. 1998. Modernités indociles et pratiques subversives en Afrique contemporaine. *Anthropologie et Sociétés*, 22(1):3-13.

Biaya, T.K. & Omasombo, T. 1993. Social classes in Zaire today. In: Kanwkenda, M. (ed.). *Zaire what destiny?* Dakar: CODESRIA, pp. 97-127.

Biaya, T.K. 1985. La 'cuistrerie' de Mbujimayi. Structure, fonctionnement et ideologie d'une bourgeoisie africaine. *Geneve-Afrique*, XVI(1):65-84.

Biaya, T.K. 1996. La culture urbaine dans les arts populaires d'Afrique: Analyse de 'l-ambiance' zaïroise. *Revue Canadienne des Etudes Africaines*, XXX(3):345-370.

Biaya, T.K. 1998a Inventing oneself. Luba: State, citizen and ethnic power in modernity. In: Geschiere, P. & Pandey, G. (eds). *State-nationhood, citizenship and ethnicity*. Leiden: SEPHIS (sous presse).

Biaya, T.K. 1998b. Transition et rationalité—politique au Zaïre. In: Diop, M.-C. & Diouf, M. (eds). *Les succession légales en Afrique*. Dakar: CODESRIA (sous presse).

Delepchin, J. 1992. *From the Congo Free State to Zaire: 1885-1974: Towards a demystification of economic and political history*. Dakar: CODESRIA.

Ilunga-Kabongo. 1984. Déroutante Afrique ou la syncope d'un discours. *Revue Canadienne des Etudes Africaines*, 18(1): 13-28.

Kankwenda, M. 1993. The problem of the accumulation model. In: Kankwenda, M. (ed.). *Zaire, what destiny?* Dakar: CODESRIA, pp. 243-263.

Kanza, T. 1977. *The rise and fall of Patrice Lumumba*. Cambridge: Schenkman.

Kinkela, V.K. 1993. Rapport final des travaux de la Conférence nationale souveraine. *Zaïre-Afrique*, 273:135-199.

MacGaffey, J. 1987. *Entrepreneurs and parasites. The struggle for indigenous capitalism in Zaire*. Cambridge: Cambridge University Press.

MacGaffey, J. 1982. The policy of national integration in Zaire. *Journal of Modern Africa Studies*, XX(2):263-285.

MacGaffey, J. 1992. Initiatives de la base: L'autre cheminement social du Zaïre et la restructuration économique. In: Hyden, G. & Bratton, M. (dir). *Gouverner l'Afrique: Vers un partage des r(tm)les*. Paris: Noueaux Horizons, pp. 345-372.

Mamdani, M. 1996. *Citizen and subject. Contemporary Africa and the legacy of late colonialism*. Princeton: Princeton University Press.

Scott, J. 1985. *Weapons of the weak: Everyday forms of peasant resistance*. New Haven: Yale University Press.

Verhaegen, B. 1978. Impérialisme technologique et bourgeoisie nationale au Zaïre. In: Coquery-Vidrovitch, C. (dir.). *Connaissance du Tiers Monde. Cahiers Jussieu*, No. 4:347-379.

Wamba-dia-Wamba, E. 1993. Democracy, multipartyism and emancipative politics in Africa: The case of Zaire. *Africa Development*, XVIII(4):95-118.

Willame, J.C. 1992. *L'automne d'un despotisme. Pouvoir, argent et obéissance dans le Zaïre des anneés quatre-vingt*. Paris: Karthala.

Chapter 5

Ethnic Identification in the Great Lakes Region

Georges Nzongola-Ntalaja

Introduction

Of all the major geographical areas of Africa, the Great Lakes region has paid the highest price in both human lives and material destruction as a result of ethnic conflict. In addition to the genocide of 1994 in Rwanda, the region has witnessed several episodes of inter-ethnic massacres since 1959. No other area of the continent has suffered as much through ethnic identity construction and mobilisation. This chapter attempts to offer a critical assessment of the role of ethnic identity construction and mobilisation as a source of conflict in the Great Lakes region. The history of ethnic identity politics in Rwanda and Burundi since the emergence of party politics in the struggle for independence provides the factual basis for the analysis.[1] The lessons of the Hutu-Tutsi confrontation for identity-based conflicts in Africa will be drawn in the conclusion.

The construction of ethnic identity in Rwanda and Burundi

Rwanda and Burundi are two of the major pre-colonial kingdoms to have survived European conquest and occupation as more or less viable political entities in Africa. From 1898 until Germany's defeat in World War I, the two territories formed part of German East Africa, which also included the mainland portion of present-day Tanzania. Having occupied Rwanda and Burundi in 1916, Belgium in 1921 formally took over their administration as a mandatory power under the League of Nations mandates system, and remained as the administrative authority under the United Nations trusteeship system from 1945 to 1962.

Although Belgium had to submit annual reports on its administration of the trust territory to the United Nations, and also had to deal with periodic inspections from the UN Trusteeship Council, the territory was already administratively annexed to the Belgian Congo in 1925. Thus, from then on until Congolese independence in 1960, Belgium governed the three territorial units as a single colonial entity known as *"Le Congo Belge et le Ruanda-Urundi"*, with a single army, the *"Force Publique"*, a single governor-general in Kinshasa, and two lieutenant governors-general—one in Lubumbashi, capital of the settler-dominated Katanga province, and the other in Bujumbura, the capital of Ruanda-Urundi.

Belgian colonialism was characterised by a close working alliance between the state, the Roman Catholic Church and large business enterprises, particularly the mining companies. Born out of the brutal legacy of primitive accumulation by the Leopoldian state and con-cessionary companies,[2] the colonial trinity sought to impose its hegemony through paternalism, white supremacy and administratively enforced ethnic divisions among Africans. The Hutu-Tutsi conflict is in large part a result of the grafting of the colonial ideology of racism and paternalism on the pre-colonial social system of both Rwanda and Burundi.

Unlike the typical ethnic map in Africa, this system was unique in that three social groups identifiable in part by differences in physical characteristics and interrelated through clientship ties, shared the same homeland, language and culture. Although the distinctions in status and occupation tended to go hand in hand with differences in physical characteristics, the social cleavages thus created were never rigid, since they were not based on differences of race, caste or religion. As the whole social order revolved around the institutions of kingdom and the patron-client relations associated with them, proximity and/or service to the royal court and its representatives in the provinces were an overriding factor in an individual's rank, whether the latter was Hutu, Tutsi or Twa.

The Twa are a pygmoid people, who also have important settlements west of the Great Lakes in the equatorial forest of Central Africa, including the nearby Ituri Forest in the Democratic Republic of the Congo (DRC). As hunter-gatherers, and undoubtedly the first occupants of the territory before its settlement by the Bantu, they were renowned for their martial skills and musical talents. This explains the important roles they played as soldiers in the king's regiments and as entertainers at the royal court. Thus, in spite of the low status and social discrimination that were the lot of the Twa as a group, male individuals could gain titles of nobility and wives of royal blood. In the traditional system, these ennobled Twa became "Tutsi". Today, the Twa are said to represent about 1% of the population in each country, as against 14% for the Tutsi and 85% for the Hutu.[3]

The Hutu occupied an intermediate position on the social pyramid— as agriculturalists and clients of Tutsi chiefs and nobles. They were also recruited into the army and in other areas of public service. Owing perhaps to the fact that they had settled in both countries before their Tutsi compatriots, there were many among them who held the position of land chief, one of the many subordinate chiefly roles in the traditional system. Like the Twa, ennobled Hutu men took daughters of Tutsi aristocrats for wives. Intermarriage between Hutu and Tutsi as part of patron-client ties and, more generally, social climbing for the Hutu, has progressively led to the decreasing importance of physical characteristics as a reliable guide for distinguishing between Hutu and Tutsi today.

The 1994 genocide and its aftermath have revived interest in the debate concerning Tutsi origins. Impressed by the social, political and military organisation of ancient Rwanda and Burundi, 19th century European adventurers and missionaries invented "theories" that resulted in the construction of a cultural mythology about the Tutsi. Among the origins attributed to them by their Western admirers were the following: (1) descendants of ancient Egyptians; (2) black Caucasians of "Hamitic" or "Semitic" origin; (3) survivors from the lost continent of Atlantis; (4) immigrants from Melanesia, Tibet, India or Asia Minor; and (5) according to one highly imaginative Catholic priest, people who came out of the Garden of Eden. Of all these labels, it was the *Hamitic* myth that stood out, partly because of its importance in colonial anthropology, and partly because of its systematisation and popularisation by a Rwandan Catholic priest, Alexis Kagame.[4]

Generally, the Tutsi were cattle owners, many of whom were associated with the royal court and the territorial expansion of its power throughout the land. Obviously, all the Tutsi were not of noble rank— there were poor and ordinary Tutsi as well—and all cattle owners were not Tutsi. In her study of Kinyaga, a peripheral region in southwestern Rwanda, Catharine Newbury points out that cattle owners who would have been considered Tutsi in central Rwanda, had arrived in Kinyaga during the 18th century. For the people of Kinyaga, however, being "Tutsi" was "associated with central government power and institutions, and particularly with the exactions of chiefs backed by central government." With the intensification of oppression under colonialism, ethnic categories came to be even more rigidly defined, while the disadvantages of being Hutu and the advantages of being Tutsi increased significantly. Passing from one ethnic category to the other was not impossible, but over time it became exceedingly difficult and, consequently, very rare.

According to René Lemarchand, "ethnic identities are not pure invention" and the social categories *Hutu* and *Tutsi* "are not figments of the colonial imagination." This is to say that although these identities have been invested with a normative load which they did not have before colonialism, the potential for ethnic mobilisation and conflict was inherent in the historically grounded relations of inequality within the precolonial social order. What the colonial system did was to take advantage of these relations by making them more rigid, and then to help intensify the antagonism between the privileged Tutsi and the disadvantaged Hutu. The Belgian colonialists effectively *ended the internal dynamic of social equilibrium* by which individuals could pass from one social category to the other, including the mechanism of ennoblement—through administrative acts and practices such as the issuance of identity cards with ethnic labels and preferential treatment for the Tutsi with respect to education, and through white-collar jobs and chiefly positions in local colonial administration.

Having served as faithful auxiliaries of the colonial order for more than 30 years, the Tutsi *elite* became expendable when its members began to advocate self-determination and independence in the 1950s. The missionaries, colonial anthropologists and other Belgian ideologues who had created the myth of Tutsi superiority, suddenly found it expedient to portray the Tutsi as an aristocracy of alien origins that should relinquish power to the oppressed Hutu indigenous majority. Although there is no evidence of systematic violence between Tutsi and Hutu during the pre-colonial period, this ideological reconstruction of their history sought to depict them as antagonistic groups with centuries-old enmities. Unfortunately, just as the old myth of Tutsi superiority had fallen on receptive ears among the Tutsi *elíte*, the new myth of Hutu as "slaves in need of emancipation" was warmly embraced by the rising Hutu counter-*elite* in its quest for the social advantages to which Hutu intellectuals felt entitled.

The process of ethnic identity construction and mobilisation thus gave rise to a dichotomous vision of society that had not existed in pre-colonial Rwanda and Burundi. If the Tutsi, like the Twa, have non-Bantu origins, the same cannot be said of the political and cultural institutions within which relations between all three groups were articulated. It is so that the monarchy that governed them, the cultural matrix in which they lived, and the language they spoke well, were all of Bantu creation and indigenous to the Great Lakes region. It is for this reason that contemporary scholarship maintains that whatever their past origins might be, the Tutsi are a Bantu people by virtue of the fact that they share a common Bantu culture with the Hutu, with whom they speak a common Bantu language, *Kinyarwanda* or *Kirundi*, depending on the country.

However, this commonality of language and culture has failed to stem the rise of an ethnic consciousness nurtured in the competition for power and privilege between Hutu and Tutsi *elites*, and to put an end to a catastrophic process of ethnic mobilisation involving *"final solution"* scenarios of genocide in both Rwanda and Burundi. It is to that history of ethnic identity politics as a source of conflict in each of these countries that we now turn.

Ethnic conflict and genocide in Rwanda

The rise of Hutu ethnic consciousness as a political force in Rwanda resulted from the emergence of a Hutu counter-*elite* in the midst of a divorce between the colonialists and their erstwhile Tutsi allies in the 1950s. The Roman Catholic Church played a key role in this process, as the new sympathies of the white clergy for the Hutu made the Church shift its support from the Tutsi *elite* to the Hutu, whom it sought to help build a new middle class. In the context of the then ongoing struggle for decolonisation and independence, economic and social advancement for Africans ultimately implied the conquest of political power.

The flexing of Hutu political muscle began in earnest in 1957. On 24 March, in anticipation of an inspection visit by the UN Trusteeship Council, nine Hutu intellectuals published a *"Hutu manifesto"* in which they denounced a political, economic and social monopoly by the Tutsi, and rejected the ideal of abolishing ethnic labels on identity papers. "Their suppression", they argue, "runs the risk of *preventing the statistical law to account for the reality of the facts"*. This is the intellectual origin of the idea of identifying democracy and majority rule with Hutu rule. Ethnically based political mobilisation for attaining this goal was launched in June and November of 1957, through the creation of two Hutu political parties—the *Mouvement social muhutu* (MSM, or Hutu Social Movement), led by a Catholic intellectual, Grégoire Kayibanda; and the *Association pour la promotion sociale de la masse* (APROSOMA, or Association for Mass Social Promotion), established by a businessman, Joseph Gitera.

Of the two men it was Kayibanda who succeeded in mobilising the masses for fulfilling the dream of a Hutu republic. Between 1952 and 1956, he served as secretary of the *Amitiés Belgo-Congolaises*, the discussion circles of Europeans and educated Africans known as the *évolués*, and as editor of a Catholic monthly, *L'Ami*. In 1956, he became editor of an influential Catholic weekly, *Kinyamateka*, and also served as private secretary to Monsignor André Perraudin, the Swiss vicar apostolic of Rwanda. With strong support from the Roman Catholic Church and Belgian colonial authorities, Kayibanda became a major opponent of Tutsi royalists, who organised themselves in 1959 under the banner of a political party, the *Union nationale rwandaise* (UNAR, or Rwandan National Union). Furthermore in 1959 Kayibanda renamed the MSM as *Mouvement démocratique rwandais/Parti du mouvement de l'émancipation hutu* (MDR-PARMEHUTU, or Rwandan Democratic Movement/Party for the Emancipation of the Hutu).

Before these and other parties were created in August-September 1959, signs of the colonial order's complicity in anti-Tutsi activities were evident in the support that individuals like Kayibanda enjoyed in official and church circles. In February of that year, the Lenten pastoral of Monsignor Perraudin on charity, in which he pleaded for social justice, was widely interpreted as a clear political choice in favor of the Hutu. With the Belgian Congo moving towards independence and the future of Rwanda and Burundi being considered in Brussels and at the United Nations in New York, the crystallisation of ethnic tensions intensified unrelentingly. In this context, the death on 25 July 1959, under mysterious circumstances, of Mwami Mutara Rudahigwa,[5] and the controversial choice of Kigeri Ndahidurwa as his successor to the Rwandan throne by conservative Tutsi elements, acted as a catalyst in the Hutu-Tutsi conflict.

The explosion came in November 1959, with the Hutu uprising generally known as the "Rwandan Revolution". This was a peculiar "revolution" in that it took place under colonialism and yet left the basic colonial or white power structure intact. Moreover, it happened not only under the watch of colonial officials, but also with their tacit consent and support. For example, it is reported that "Belgian authorities were very partial in the favor of the Hutu, letting them burn Tutsi houses without intervening." Furthermore, the colonial authorities rewarded Hutu violence by installing mostly Hutu administrators in the communes, to replace the Tutsi chiefs and administrators who had either been killed or fled.

To the people of Rwanda the events of November 1959 were truly revolutionary, in the sense that they ultimately resulted in the overthrow of the monarchy and the transfer of political power from one ethnic group to the other. In Kinyarwanda, what happened is referred to as the "*muyaga*", a word normally used to describe a strong but variable wind, with unpredictable and destructive gusts. Although independence came nearly three years later, on 1 July 1962, the basic framework of the Hutu republic was already being established in 1959. Another major consequence of the *muyaga* was the large number of refugees and internally displaced persons it generated. At the time of independence, the number of refugees in the neighbouring countries and abroad was estimated at about 120 000.

The number of refugees continued to grow, due to both natural increase and new outflows resulting from episodic outbursts of inter-ethnic violence and the politics of exclusion practised by both Kayibanda and his successor, Juvénal Habyarimana. A career army officer who had quit medical school at Lovanium University in Kinshasa to enrol in the newly created Rwandan army in 1960, Habyarimana overthrew President Kayibanda in 1973 and subsequently established a military and one-party dictatorship. In over 20 years of personal rule, he steadfastly refused to allow Tutsi refugees to return home. In August 1988, a world congress of the Tutsi diaspora was held in Washington, DC, with delegates adopting very strong resolutions on the "right of return". Meanwhile, the Tutsi diaspora in Uganda had gained positions of responsibility and influence in Yoweri Museveni's National Resistance Army (NRA), after having helped the latter come to power in Kampala in January 1986. Under the leadership of the Rwandese Patriotic Front (RPF), the group launched a military offensive in October 1990, to overthrow the Habyarimana regime. France, Belgium and Mobutu's Zaire came to the dictator's rescue and prevented an RPF victory.

Under the auspices of the Organisation of African Unity (OAU) and sub-regional actors, negotiations—over two years—between Habyarimana's government and the RPF—to end the civil war, led to the signing of the Arusha accords in 1993. These included the Arusha Peace Agreement of 4 August 1993, a cease-fire agreement, and six protocols on a variety of subjects, including the rule of law, power sharing, integration of the two armed forces, repatriation of refugees and resettlement of displaced persons. In spite of having signed these accords, President Habyarimana did his best to undermine them, and thus played into the hands of Hutu extremists bent on exterminating the Tutsi.

The shooting down of Habyariman's plane on 6 April 1994 gave these extremists the opportunity they needed to unleash their genocidal machine against the Tutsi and the Hutu moderates who were campaigning for democratisation and national reconciliation. Planned in advance by advocates of *Hutu Power*, which involved the President's wife and her brothers, the genocide was carried out with military precision over a three-month period, with some 800 000 to one million people killed. With the United Nations and the entire world looking on without doing anything to stop it, the holocaust ended only in the wake of the victory of the RPF over Habyarimana's army, the *Forces armées rwandaises* (FAR).

Once the RPF victory seemed certain, France obtained UN approval for a supposedly "humanitarian intervention" in Rwanda. If we must acknowledge the good deeds of its soldiers in caring for and burying cholera victims in Kivu, it is imperative to affirm that there was nothing humanitarian in France's intent, given its own role as an accessory to crime in Rwanda. As Jean-François Médard, a renowned French Africanist, told *Newsweek* magasine in 1994, French policy in Africa was "erratic and criminal", as Paris operated "not on principle, but on cynicism." The cynicism was evident in that having supported the Habyarimana regime and trained its genocidal machine, including the extremist Hutu *Interahamue* militia, the French were more anxious to erase the traces of their own involvement in Rwanda by rescuing their former allies, than in helping the victims of genocide inside the country. In April the French had evacuated regime dignitaries, including known organisers of the genocide, while even Tutsi employees of the French Embassy were left behind to be killed. Through the *Opération Turquoise* (June-August 1994), the French succeeded in helping the FAR and the *Interahamue* escape into the Congo with virtually all of the weapons at their disposal. This allowed these groups to regroup for purposes of reconquering Rwanda and finishing off their genocidal enterprise.

The genociders then used the refugee camps in Kivu to raid Rwanda on a regular basis, and to organise the slaughter of Tutsi citizens and residents of the Congo. For two and a half years, the Mobutu-Kengo regime and the international community watched and did nothing to stop this, while the UN and the donor community continued to be more preoccupied with feeding the refugees than trying to remove the killers among them and finding a lasting solution to the whole crisis.

In October 1996 the RPF regime took the initiative to destroy the UNHCR refugee camps in Kivu and, consequently, the bases of the FAR and *Interahamue* in the Congo. The victorious march of Laurent-Désiré Kabila, and his *Alliance des forces démocratiques pour la libération du Congo* (AFDL), could not have taken place without the RPF drive against the genociders. The alleged massacres of Hutu non-combatants (old men, women and children) during the seven-month war against the Mobutu regime remain a hotly debated subject, whose resolution should provide answers with respect to the prospects for peace and national reconciliation in Rwanda.

Ethnicity and genocidal violence in Burundi

As mentioned earlier, the roots of the Hutu-Tutsi confrontation in both Rwanda and Burundi are to be found in the ideological reconstruction of history by Christian missionaries and colonial anthropologists, as well as in its appropriation by Africans in the competition for power and privilege between Tutsi and Hutu *elites*. Rwandans and Burundians insist, and with reason, that theirs are two separate countries, with different social realities, and should therefore not be confused as one and the same entity. However, given the similarity in the ethnic make-up as well as in ethnic identity construction and mobilisation, it is hard to imagine that events in one country would not affect developments in the other. In fact, every major event, from the *muyaga* of 1959 to the genocide of 1994 in Rwanda, and from the inter-ethnic massacres of 1972 to those of 1993 in Burundi, has had a tremendous mutual impact across the border in the neighbouring country.

Unlike Rwanda, where the Tutsi-dominated monarchy was overthrown in 1959, Burundi achieved independence in 1962—as a constitutional monarchy—with Mwami Mwambutsa IV as head of state. At the same time, the impact of the Hutu revolution in Rwanda was greatly felt there. According to Lemarchand, "no other event did more to sharpen the edges of ethnic hatreds in Burundi" at that time, since the respective positions of Hutu and Tutsi leaders were by and large shaped by what happened in Rwanda.

In the months following independence, a number of Hutu politicians began to feel the contagion of republican ideas. By identifying their political aims and aspirations with their Rwandan kinsmen, they imputed to the Tutsi of Burundi hegemonic motives that the Tutsi did not at first possess, but to which they eventually gave a substance of truth. Conversely, many Tutsi saw in the Rwanda upheaval an ominous prefiguration of their own destinies. A kind of self-fulfilling prophecy was thus set in motion: by giving the Burundi situation a false definition to begin with, Hutu and Tutsi politicians evoked a new set of attitudes among each other, which made their originally false imputations true.

Much of the history of Burundi in the last 36 years has consisted of a succession of events whose practical outcome seems to underscore this prophecy. However, such a trajectory was not inevitable, inasmuch as Burundi had a chance of avoiding ethnically based political polarisation à la Rwanda. Unlike Rwanda, political life there was not originally ordered along ethnic lines, when party politics began in the late 1950s. The most serious crisis to mark the country on the eve of independence, was the assassination on 13 October 1961 of Prince Louis Rwagasore. Eldest son of Mwami Mwambutsa, and one of the founding fathers of the major nationalist party, *Parti de l'union et du progrès national* (UPRONA, or Party of Unity and National Progress), Prince Rwagasore was equally popular among Hutu and Tutsi. As Prime Minister designate after his party had won the legislative elections of September 1961, he was assassinated in a conflict between two *Ganwa* princely families dating back to the 19th century.[6] If there is one leader who embodied national unity, and who had the credibility needed to steer Burundi away from the Rwanda model, it was Prince Rwagasore.[7]

The next four years were to witness the heightening of ethnic tensions in the context of continuing turmoil in Rwanda, the Congo crisis, and the geopolitical considerations of the cold war associated with it. The influx of Tutsi refugees from Rwanda kept alive the seduction of the Rwanda model for some Hutu leaders, while solidifying opposition to it among the Tutsi *elite*. The turning point came in 1965, with the assassination in January of Prime Minister Pierre Ngendandumwe, a Hutu; the attempted *coup d'état* by Hutu officers, and its bitter aftermath.

Like Rwagasore, Ngendandumwe exemplified the political will among some Tutsi and Hutu intellectuals to work together for the good of the country. The first Hutu university graduate in Burundi, he was Rwagasore's right hand man in UPRONA and deputy prime minister. A year after Rwagasore's death, he succeeded the latter's brother-in-law, André Muhirwa, as prime minister. After two years in power, he was assassinated by a Rwandan Tutsi refugee employed in the accounting section of the US Embassy in Bujumbura. The assailant, who was obviously a hired gun, had no difficulty escaping, to live as a free person in Uganda. The assassination was perceived as an ethnically inspired political liquidation, and taken by most of the Hutu as conclusive proof that the Tutsi did not trust or want them in positions of power in Burundi.

This position was reinforced by the crises that followed. In the wake of Ngendandumwe's assassination, the legislative elections of May 1965 were a kind of ethnic plebiscite. Of the total of 33 seats in the National Assembly, Hutu politicians won 23 and expected therefore to lead the government. The Crown decided otherwise, with Mwami Mwambutsa appointing Léopold Biha, a long time protégé of the royal court, as prime minister. The resulting impasse put the whole parliamentary system on trial: for the Tutsi minority, the system excluded them from meaningful political participation, while for the Hutu majority, its manipulation by the Crown and the Tutsi elite, pointed to the latter's rejection of the legitimacy of the ballot box. A group of Hutu military officers then attempted a *coup d'état* on 19 October 1965. Its failure resulted not only in extensive purges in the army and the *gendarmerie*, but also in the physical elimination of nearly all prominent Hutu leaders, and the establishment of an exclusive monopoly of power by the Tutsi. All of the inter-ethnic massacres since then, were related to the determination of some Tutsi elements to maintain this monopoly at all costs, and that of Hutu politicians, to destroy it. For some, maintaining or destroying this monopoly required the use of all means necessary, including genocide.

The genocidal character of inter-ethnic violence in Burundi was clearly evident in the momentous events of 1972. In April a Hutu rebellion broke out in the southern part of the country, with several thousand Tutsi men, women and children massacred. The repression by the Tutsi power structure was merciless. The army, backed up by the youth branch of the ruling single party, went after Hutu intellectuals and other middle class elements, including high school students, who were targeted on the assumption that they were likely to join the middle class in the future. Moderate Tutsi elements were also targeted, either as part of intra-Tutsi rivalries, or because they were seen as threatening the maintenance of Tutsi hegemony. Estimates of people killed—in what observers have called a "selective genocide"—range from 100 000 to 350 000, in a population of 3 to 4 million people. What happened in 1972 was repeated on a smaller scale in 1988 in the north, as the army's response to killings of Tutsi by Hutu peasants resulted in over 10 000 people killed.[8]

The 1988 inter-ethnic massacres occurred at a time when a new wind of change was beginning to sweep across the continent. In Burundi itself, Major Pierre Buyoya had staged a *coup d'état* against President Jean-Baptiste Bagaza in 1987. He designated a Hutu prime minister, in an effort to move towards power sharing and national reconciliation, and went forward with the plan to liberalise the political system. In spite of a new episode of inter-ethnic massacres in November 1991, resulting from a terrorist attack by an extremist Hutu exile group—the *Parti pour la libération du peuple hutu* (PALIPEHUTU, or Party for the Liberation of Hutu People)—the democratisation process went ahead until general elections in June 1993. The elections were won by a new political party, the *Front pour la démocratie au Burundi* (FRODEBU, or Front for Democracy in Burundi). Its Hutu leader, Melchior Ndadaye, became Burundi's first democratically elected president.

A national party open to all groups, FRODEBU was perceived as being essentially a Hutu political party. According to Christian Thibon, its social basis was made up mostly of the lower stratum of the Hutu middle class, particularly school teachers, lower-level civil servants and the lowest ranks in the military (corporals and enlisted men). These are groups which had been frustrated by the lack of promotion and social advancement due to the Tutsi-imposed social closure. In the rural areas, these groups had a real constituency amongst the peasantry, particularly among younger elements. With so many Hutu professionals and intellectuals already eliminated in genocidal violence, many of Ndadaye's collaborators came from the lower middle class. Consequently, in spite of President Ndadaye's attempt to reassure everyone that he was committed to national reconciliation, a proportion of both the army and the Tutsi *elite* did not trust him, seeing his administration as representing a potential shift of political control from the Tutsi to the Hutu. Ndadaye and many of his associates were assassinated on 21 October 1993, 100 days after taking office.

A new wave of inter-ethnic massacres followed. Hutu wrath was directed not only at the Tutsi, but also at Hutu members of the UPRONA. As usual, the army's intervention to protect the Tutsi resulted in the extermination of thousands of people and the generation of over 500 000 refugees and 100 000 internally displaced persons. After nearly three years of a confused political situation—but one marked by an intensifying armed conflict between the Tutsi-controlled army and exiled Hutu movements like PALIPEHUTU and the *Conseil national pour la défense de la démocratie* (CNDD, or National Council for the Defense of Democracy)— Major Buyoya staged another *coup d'état* in July 1996. Having lost the presidential election of 1993 to Ndadaye, he was then negotiating with FRODEBU and other parties to move the country forward on the path of power-sharing and national reconciliation.

Conclusion

The Hutu-Tutsi conflict is an excellent example of how identities are constructed and manipulated in particular circumstances, with deadly results in the long run if the social divide is allowed to deepen and fester. As a particularly violent form of social polarisation and antagonism, it belongs to a type of conflict based on racial, regional, ethnic, religious or communal ties. *Identity-based conflicts*, as they are commonly known, may involve the struggle for physical space as well as social well-being, and have to do with both the biological needs for food, shelter and clothing, and the socio-psychological needs for identity, security, recognition, participation and autonomy. Ignoring or suppressing such basic human needs is likely to give rise to violent conflicts.[9]

The question that readily comes to mind, is why violent conflicts should result from antagonism between groups based on differences in identity. What is it about communal, ethnic, racial, regional or religious differences that drives human beings to kill and maim each other? Contrary to the modernisation theory's thesis of primordial sentiments, identity-based conflicts are not necessarily a function of ancient enmities. Since identities are *historically constructed*, they may shift with changing circumstances. Moreover, there is a lot of social science evidence that identity ties and sentiments are situational, which is to say that their intensity varies according to circumstances. In situations of relative security, an individual or a group's identity is not a matter of particular concern. It is when a threat arises, or is perceived to be such—aimed against a group's identity or its very existence because of that identity— that loyalty to, and solidarity with fellow group members becomes paramount.

In Africa many of the identities behind present-day ethnic conflicts arose or acquired their specific saliency during the colonial period. Often, as in the case of Rwanda and Burundi, ethnic identity construction and mobilisation were tied to both the colonial strategy of "divide and rule", and intra-*elite* competition for status, wealth and power among educated Africans. In the postwar struggle for social advancement first, and decolonisation and independence later on, the ability of the *évolués to* score points against their colonial masters depended greatly on how well they could mobilise the masses behind their social and political demands. Getting the support of the urban masses for these demands required very little effort, as wage workers and the *lumpen-proletariat* did interact with their more educated kith and kin, through ethnically based mutual aid associations. The more difficult task was ethnic consciousness raising in the countryside, which often required the dispatching of "ethnic missionaries" to spread the gospel of group solidarity and social upliftment in the rural homeland.

In Rwanda and Burundi, where the rival ethnic groups do not have separate homelands, consciousness raising occurs as armed propaganda, as individuals are challenged to prove their ethnic "worth" in deeds—by killing the enemy. By this token, the conflict goes beyond communal violence over economic and social space, which involves the destruction of crops, livestock and dwellings, to ethnic cleansing and, finally group extermination. The genocide ideology inherent in this process is the logical conclusion of the survival strategy born out of real or perceived threats to group identity and security. The logic here is a simple one: you either eliminate "the other"—or take the risk of being eliminated by them. The other is also demonised as the incarnation of all evil, and animalised by portraying them as "insects", "cockroaches" or other creatures. Once dehumanised in this way, the hated group can be exterminated without the risk of this odious act incurring any moral problems for its perpetrators.

The situational character of identity-based conflicts calls for greater attention to the economic and political crises that exacerbate them. For these conflicts are ultimately related to the nature and role of the state in post-colonial Africa, including the state's role in the economy, and the manner in which state power is exercised. In other words, their root causes are to be found in the economic sphere and in governance.

In the four decades of independence the economic and social structures that reproduce poverty have remained intact. The economic conditions deteriorated greatly during the 1980s, due to unfavourable terms of trade, increase in real interest rates on the external debt, reduced inflow of resources, and massive capital outflows. This led to declines in domestic investment and government consumption, resulting in a decrease in the productive capacity and growth potential of African economies, as well as the neglect of social and economic services such as roads, energy, health-care facilities, education, research, agricultural extension and credit programmes. The consequences of all this today include an unfavourable adjustment in the incomes of most social groups. The rural areas have experienced declines in real incomes and serious deterioration in the availability of public services and consumer goods. In the urban sector, wage and salary workers have been hardest hit by both retrenchment and a more hostile work environment in which private employers and the state alike are taking advantage of massive unemployment to impose low wages and unsatisfactory working conditions.

In the political sphere the state operates mostly as the "property" of those who hold political power and their entourage, rather than as an impartial system of institutions serving the general interest. This "privatisation" of the state, together with the resulting failure to fulfil the people's aspirations for democracy and economic development, has led to the erosion of its legitimacy and a reduced capacity for good governance. The crisis of the state thus creates an environment in which violent conflicts are likely to thrive. Whereas the breakdown of state authority creates a power vacuum that different political forces may use to advance their own agendas, the erosion of state legitimacy often compels authoritarian rulers to unleash a violent backlash against the forces advocating democratic change. When the power holders themselves are defined primarily as regionally or ethnically based groups, political exclusion becomes a major ground for fighting the system. This was the case for the Tutsi minority in Rwanda until 1994, and for the Hutu majority in Burundi since independence, except for the 100 days of the Ndadaye presidency.

Thus, the very nature of the state as a regionally, or, in this case, an ethnically defined monopoly of power, is a major factor in such identity based conflict. Since the state is still the primary avenue of wealth accumulation and the principal employer of wage labour in most African countries, maintaining access to the state and the resources it controls is a major goal for individuals and social groups. As John Markakis has pointed out in his study of conflict in the Horn of Africa, access to the state and state-controlled resources is the bone of contention in class and ethnic conflicts in Africa. With the state as a "prise", the parties to the conflict engage in a deadly zero-sum game, and resort to violence as the most effective means for winning and keeping the prise.

However, the use of violence leads to the destruction of existing capacity and to the further erosion of state legitimacy among the losers, who are likely to be excluded from power and state-controlled resources. Violent conflicts have unleashed untold suffering on millions of innocent men, women and children, and entailed heavy costs for the countries involved as well as their neighbours, who must cope with the problem of refugees. The destruction of the natural environment, the physical infrastructure and invaluable social services, has further reduced the capacity of the state and the economy to meet the most basic human needs. A major "cause" of conflict, poverty is also its inevitable result.

For Africa, the major lesson of the Hutu-Tutsi conflict in particular, and identity-based conflicts in general, is to avoid the politics of exclusion. Given the relatively low level of economic and social development in the continent, finding innovative methods of power sharing and ensuring access to the state and state-controlled resources for all relevant social forces, are categorical imperatives for peace and security in the foreseeable future. Patriotic and Pan-African forces should do their utmost to promote national reconciliation and to help prevent or resolve violent conflicts. Containing identity-based conflicts within the arena of non-violent political competition is a necessary condition for building multi-ethnic political coalitions and strengthening the institutional foundations of economic recovery and good governance.

Notes

[1] For a brief analysis of the repercussions of the Hutu-Tutsi conflict in the Democratic Republic of the Congo, and the related issues of the *Banyarwanda* and *Banyamulenge* in North and South Kivu, see Georges Nzongola-Ntalaja, 1996. "Africa Focus: Conflict in Eastern Zaire", *Africa Insight*, Vol. 26, No. 43, pp. 392-394.

[2] Between 1885 and 1908, the Congo was theoretically an independent country, the Congo Free State, under the rule of King Léopold II of the Belgians. The only freedom that existed then was for Léopold and his agents to plunder the

country as they saw fit, while committing, in the process, atrocities that were denounced internationally as crimes against humanity.

[3] Widely accepted as such, these population estimates are suspect, because of their fixed and unchanging nature.

[4] On Alexis Kagame and his influence as a historian of ancient Rwanda, see Catharine Newbury. 1988. *The Cohesion of Oppression: Clientship and Ethnicity in Rwanda, 1860-1960*. New York: Columbia University Press. Note 13, pp. 247-248; Prunier, 1977, pp. 52-53.

[5] *Mwami* or *umwami* is the commonly used word for king in most of the traditional political systems of the Great Lakes region.

[6] See Christian Thibon, "Les origines historiques de la violence politique au Burundi," in André Guichaoua (Ed.) 1995. *Les crises politiques au Burundi et au Rwanda (1993-1994)*. Lille: Université de Lille 1, p. 56. According to Lemarchand (*Burundi*, p. 10), the *ganwa* or ruling princely oligarchy originally formed "a separate ethnic entity different from both Hutu and Tutsi". Under the colonial system, however, the group became identified with the Tutsi.

[7] There seems to be universal agreement on this point among Burundian intellectuals and foreign experts. See Lemarchand, *Burundi*, p. 26; Sebudandi and Richard, *Le drame burundais*, p. 173; Thibon, "Les origines historiques", p. 56.

[8] Estimates range from 5 000 to 15 000 people killed. For a detailed analysis of the differences between 1972 and 1988, see Lemarchand, *Burundi*, pp. 118-130.

[9] On the socio-psychological dimension of identity-based conflicts, see Okwudiba Nnoli, 1989. *Ethnic Politics in Africa*. Apapa, Lagos: AAPS Books, pp. 17-20.

References

Krop, P. 1994. *Le génocide franco-africain: Faut-il juger les Mitterand?* Paris: Editions Jean-Claude Lattès.

Lemarchand, R. 1996. *Burundi: Ethnic conflict and genocide.* New York: Woodrow Wilson Press and Cambridge University Press.

Markakis, J. 1987. *National and class conflict in the Horn of Africa.* Cambridge: Cambridge University Press.

Markakis, J. 1991. The bone of contention in the Horn of Africa. In: Nzongola-Ntalaja, G. (ed.). *Conflict in the Horn of Africa*. Atlanta: African Studies Association Press, pp. 19-25.

Nnoli, O. 1989. *Ethnic politics in Africa*. Apapa, Lagos: AAPS Books.

Nzongola-Ntalaja, G. 1985. The national question and the crisis of instability in Africa. *Alternatives*, 10(4): 548, Special UN Commemorative Issue.

Prunier, G. 1977. *Rwanda, 1959-1996: Histoire d'un génocide*. Paris: Dagorno.

Sebudandi, G. & Richard, P-O. 1996. *Le drame burundais: Hantise du pouvoir ou tentation suicidaire*. Paris: Karthala.

Thibon, C. 1995. Les origines historiques de la violence politique au Burundi. In: Guichaoua, A. (ed.). *Les crises politiques au Burundi et au Rwanda (1993-1994)*. Lille: Université de Lille 1.

Chapter 6

Ethno-religious Nationalism in Sudan: The Enduring Constraint on the Policy of National Identity

Korwa G. Adar

Introduction

Attempts by the Sudanese administrations since 1956 to establish a workable and legitimate constitutional framework embracing the interests of the over 570 heterogeneous citizenry groups in Sudan have remained an elusive project. Instead, the country has been polarised into ethno-religious and territorial nationalisms, culminating into the war of attrition between the regimes in Sudan and the rebel movements since 1955. Whereas conflict in Sudan has acquired a multidimensional character over the years, the main belligerents have been the Arab-speaking Muslims of the north and the southern black Sudanese. At the core of the civil war are the inherently exclusive ethno-religious-centred policies, namely Islamisation and Arabisation pursued in various ways by successive Sudanese administrations since the 1950s. The persistent derogation of the linguistic and religio-cultural practices of the southerners and non-Muslims in general by the Arab-speaking Muslims, continues to impose limitations on the drive to establish a durable consensus on the Sudanese national identity.

The policies of Islamisation and Arabisation, with their cultural dimensions and implications, have remained the central mobilisation force and rallying point for the political survival of the Sudanese ruling *elite*. On the other side of the political spectrum is the transformation of Sudan into a theocratic state, which has forced the southern Sudanese to use ethnicity as the rallying point for their survival and security against authoritarianism and oppression by the north. The southern Sudanese resent their marginalisation by the regimes in power.[1]

The marginalisation of the southern Sudanese and the Nuba is not a recent phenomenon. It was practiced by the British colonialists and thereafter maintained by the post-independence administrations in Sudan, and thirdly, there is the ongoing discrimination, oppression and repression of the black Sudanese.[2] History therefore constitutes one of the *prima facie* determinants of conflict and ethnic polarisation between the north and the south. This is not to argue, however, that the issues of self-preservation, autonomy, and ethnic identity by the south, as the core factors underlying conflict in Sudan, are not important. The south did not accept the Anglo-Egyptian colonialism in Sudan. Similarly the southerners have not accepted the post-independence Sudanese policies of Islamisation.[3]

This chapter focuses on conflict and ethnic identity in Sudan. Specifically, it examines the extent to which ethno-religious nationalism—centralised within the context of Islamisation—imposes limitations on a nationally oriented Sudanese identity. The first part of the discussion puts into proper perspective the meaning of Islamisation, whereas the second part examines the interplay between Islamisation and religious identification and mobilisation in the Sudanese conflict. Part three puts into proper perspective the extent to which oil production in Sudan imposes limitations on conflict resolution and undermines the possibility for the establishment of a consensus on national identity. Part four focuses on the impact of Islamisation and "Sudanese national" identity. Two issues need to be clarified at the outset. First, in this study I shall treat the Southern Sudanese and people of the Nuba Mountains as one entity fighting for their rights in the Sudan. Similarly, the Arabic-speaking peoples of the north will also be treated as a single entity influenced largely by their culture and religion, Islam.[4] We do recognise that such a sharp dichotomy is problematic, in the sense that there are some black African Sudanese who live in the north. However, this approach is adopted mainly for convenience and analytical purposes. Of the more than 32 million Sudanese, the black Africans, the Arabs, and the Beja constitute

52%, 39% and 6% of the population respectively. Over 70% and 10% of the population are respectively Muslims and Christians. This study does not attempt to offer a detailed analysis of Islam and *Sharia law, per se.*

Islamisation and Arabisation: A framework for analysis

It important that the meaning of Islamisation and Arabisation be put into their proper contexts, particularly with respect to the extent to which they have been applied by Sudanese regimes. This would provide a clear understanding of the implications the policies have had on the southern Sudanese who are advocating a secular state, that is, the separation of church and state.[5] In its broad context, Arabisation simply means the process of the integration and assimilation of individuals into the cultural values and beliefs of Muslims and Arabs in particular. As a result of Arabisation and, by extension, Islamisation, northern Sudanese ethnic groups tend to produce genealogies that have historically linked them to Arab origins.[6] It is for these reasons that the ruling *elites* in Sudan have persistently incorporated Arabic culture, language and religion into the legal and political structures of the state for their political survival.[7]

Different interpretations have been advanced with respect to the meaning of Islamisation. The traditionalist thesis stresses that Islamisation is nothing other than the reintroduction of the past Islamic institutions and traditional laws which deal with different forms of punishment. These laws are to be followed to the letter with the reservation of separate facilities for men and women, and a "protected" status for non-Muslims.[8] Non-Muslims are accommodated within the context of a recognition of diversity among Muslims and society as a whole. Traditionalists recognise that there is disagreement among Muslim *ikhtilaf*, that is Islamic law did not evolve as a monolithic corpus. Disagreement also extends between Muslims and non-Muslims, or the people of the book *ahl al-kitab*, Jews and Christians. Traditionalists see themselves as the custodians of the original and "Dynamic" Islamic faith.

The reformers (neo-traditionalists) conceptualise the process of Islamisation as a dynamic development of Islam. It involves the process of interpretation and assimilation that characterise Islamic tradition, while at the same time incorporating foreign sources which do not contradict Islam.[9] This practice, according to the reformers, is not unique in Islamic law. The reformers stress that new ideas and problems can only be solved by the adoption and adaptation of new solutions prevailing at any given time. Without accepting Westernisation, the reformers, however, borrow from certain Western cultures. In Sudan, *Sadiq al-Mahdi* (Mahdism—a movement that believes in political struggle and in the establishment of an Islamic state) and *Hassan al-Turabi* (Muslim Brotherhood) represent this Islamic persuasion. The other Islamic movements that have had an influence in Sudan through their grassroots support, include the *Ansar* (followers of Mahdi), and *Khatmiyya*. The Sudanese Muslims share Sunni Islamic faith which believes "in an eschatological individual who will come in the future to deliver the community from oppression by the forces of evil and to restore true Islam and with it a reign of justice on earth".[10] These views form part of their persistent belief in the necessity of establishing an Islamic state. Before dealing with Islamisation, a brief analysis of Ansar, Khatmiyya and Muslim Brotherhood would suffice.

Although the Sudanese Mahdi state had been destroyed by the Anglo-Egyptian conquest at the end of the nineteenth century, the religious movement itself did not end. It gained greater currency under the leadership of Mahdi's son, Sayyid Abd al-Rahman, between 1885 and 1959. He organised the Mahdi followers, the Ansar, into a political force that gained influence during the Sudanese independence movement.[11] The Ansar established the Umma Party whose main objective was the unity of Sudan into an Islamic state. Khatmiyya finds its roots within the *Khatmiyya Tariqah movement*, founded by an Egyptian, Muhammad Uthman al-Mirghani (1793-1853), who travelled widely in Sudan during the period of Egyptian rule.[12] With its wide support during the drive for Sudanese independence, the movement advocated unification with Egypt. It became one of the centres of political parties in Sudan, with its platform focusing on Islamisation of the state. In 1956 Khatmiyya forces formed their own political party, the People's Democratic Party, to advocate Sudanese independence. The Muslim Brotherhood also had its roots in

Egypt. Founded in Egypt in the early 1950s by Muslims who rejected the western secular path Egypt was taking at the time, they, instead, advocated a return to Arab culture, Islam and *sharia* laws.

Although influenced by the Egyptian Muslim Brotherhood, the Sudanese Muslim Brotherhood is autonomous. The Brotherhood advocates the adoption of an Islamic socio-political system in which the Constitution is centred on the *Quran*, with *Sharia law* representing the basis of the Sudanese legal system. As with their Egyptian counterparts, the Sudanese Muslim Brotherhood rejects the westernisation and secularisation of Sudan, and instead advocates a modern Islamic state. The movement became more prominent in the 1960s under the leadership of Hassan al-Turabi. Originally operating under the banner of the Islamic Charter Front Party, the Brotherhood participated in the establishment of the National Front—a conglomeration of the Umma (Ansar) Party, the Democratic Union Party (DUP), and the Islamic Charter Front (ICF)—with Sadiq al-Mahdi as its leader. All these movements-cum-political parties stressed the need to make Sudan an Islamic state. Islamisation, therefore, became a major theme in their pronouncements.

At the core of Islamisation lie the doctrines of Islamic culture and religion. According to this view, implementation of Arabic culture, language, and religion—*Sharia*—cannot be brought about in isolation and without the concomitant internal political realities. Islamisation (read, application of *Sharia* laws) is used as a tool for political power and legitimacy.[13] Implementation of *Sharia* means conforming to the will of God, who by extension, is the sole "legislator". In this conception, human will is excluded from legislation. Thus, the law or God's will, precedes the state. The central duty of the state, therefore, is to carry out God's law.[14] To disobey the law constitutes an act which contravenes religious doctrine, and is subject to religious punishment. *Sharia*, therefore, controls and regulates socio-political and economic life which form the basis of political authority—"reinforced by the dogma of the divine guidance of the community".[15] The incorporation of *Sharia* law in a constitution offers the basis for the promotion of Islamic principles. Islamisation is therefore an important vehicle for promoting values associated with Islam and Arabic culture.

Irrespective of the fact that the *Quran* does not mention constitutionalism *per se*, constitutionalism is necessary for realising the just and good society prescribed by the *Quran*.[16] What is central here is that justification and legitimacy for the survival at the helm of the state is directly linked with prescriptions of Islamisation. In other words, Islam is *din wa dawla*, that is, Islam is "religion and state".[17] This is not to argue, however, that Islam is static or monolithic. As I have explained, the debate on the conceptions of Islamisation by the traditionalists and reformers is a continuous process. The reformers under the Muslim Brotherhood and Jamaat-I Islami, among others, advocate more participation in the political process in Muslim societies, while at the same time maintaining Islamic prescriptions. The reformers, therefore, emphasise the existence of a dual relationship between Islamisation and democratisation. The concepts of Islamisation and democratisation lie outside the scope of this discussion and will not be dealt with here.[18] One of the questions which arises, is the place of non-Muslims in a state pursuing the policy of Islamisation. I have demonstrated that there is a direct linkage, with some variants, between religion and the state, as conceived by both the traditionalists and reformers. Indeed, this linkage is necessitated because of its religious relevance and internal mass demand.

Islamisation has a number of implications for non-Muslims. In the early centuries of Islamic conquest, non-Muslims were subjugated to Muslim rule, with the *jihad* (holy war) being used as a means of controlling territory under Muslim jurisdiction, as well as to conquer more areas. The conquered people were not forced to convert to Islam because that is against *Sharia* laws. The use of *jihad* is not a common phenomenon in contemporary interstate relations. This is not to argue, however, that contemporary Muslim political leaders do not use it as a tool for mobilisation and propaganda if they are faced with internal or external threats.

In the pre-modern period, non-Muslims, particularly Christians and Jews who submitted to Muslim rule, were given the status of *dhimmis*.

These were contracts concluded between Muslims and non-Muslims which accorded the latter protection, provided that they accepted the domination of Islam. The non-Muslims (Jews and Christians) were to pay *jizya* (special tax) and were exempted from serving in the military, but were instead subject to *Sharia* law.[19] The *jizya* was regarded either as "compensation for being spared from death ... [or] for living in Muslim land."[20] These contractual arrangements were not extended to communities regarded by Muslims as polytheist—those who were neither Jews nor Christians. Instead, the polytheists were given the "option" of either accepting Islam or choosing death.[21] However, Muslims were more tolerant in their treatment of religious minorities, compared with Christians. These premodern prescriptions constitute the centre of a debate in the contemporary Muslim world—comprising a population of over one billion. One of the central questions is the status of non-Muslims in a state which is pursuing Islamisation policies.

The central argument of those who subscribe to the traditional thesis is that there is no equality between Muslims and non-Muslims within and under *Sharia* law. The underlying perspective of the traditionalists is that Islamisation is therefore essential for the *ahl al-kitab*:

> Since their faith has not reached the highest level of spirituality, but obeys commands which we believe to have been abrogated, and puts other laws in place of those revealed through Islam by the means of the Prophet and most righteous Judge, therefore [the Sharia] makes certain differences between them and Muslims, treating them as not on the same level.[22]

This interpretation of *Sharia* is in conformity with the pre-modern perspectives. Tabandeh argues that those who have not accepted one God, are "outside the pale of humanity", and are to be treated as non-persons.[23] It is important to note here that non-Muslims, according to this viewpoint, are not accorded political rights and freedoms.[24]

The reformers' perspective regarding non-Muslims in relation to Muslims, is also generally tailored on *Sharia* law, with little variation.

However, non-Muslims today do not accept the second class status enshrined in the traditional conceptions of Islamisation. Whereas the issues of equality in citizenship and opportunity are stipulated in some constitutions in Islamic states, restrictions for non-Muslims still prevail because of these inherent internal pressures. Non-Muslims are not accorded the opportunity to hold key government positions because they are not fully committed to Islamic ideology.[25] Islamisation policies pursued by those who subscribe to the modernistic thesis are couched within this perspective. Control of state apparatus is therefore central both for the traditionalists *and* reformers.

A number of points need to be reiterated here to conclude this section. Firstly, both the traditionalists and reformers support policies of Islamisation, with the state functioning as a means of promoting *Sharia* law and as a source of power. In such a society, church and state have complementary and overlapping responsibilities and functions. Secondly, both perspectives disagree, for example, on some of the implications of the law *vis-à-vis* non-Muslims. Various disagreements with respect to the interpretations of *Sharia* law have existed for centuries, hence the conflicting viewpoints on Islamisation programmes.

Implications of Islamisation for religious identification, mobilisation and conflict

Sudan's stability, unity and sovereignty have been persistently threatened by its internal civil war since independence in 1956. Whereas intra-factional disagreements and conflict dating back to the 1950s occurred, the centre of the civil war has been between the Arab-speaking Muslims of the north and black Sudanese of the south. It is important first of all to underpin the aetiology and rationale of the southern Sudanese in relation to their search for a separate legitimacy and identity from the rest of Sudan. The objective here is not to give a detailed historical analysis.[26] The problem centres on the historical, socio-economic, cultural, religious, and political situation in Sudan.

The British administered the two regions as separate entities, with little economic, political and infrastructural development in the south. This evoked and enhanced southern aspirations and consciousness.[27] The formation of the Sudan African Closed Districts National Union (SACDNU) later changed to Sudan African National Union (SANU), and the Southern Front Party (SFP), changed the political scenario in Sudan. The two movements promoted and cemented southern opinion on their relations with the north. The other important factor which prompted the south to demand autonomy and identification is religion. The majority of the southerners are animists, as well as Catholics and Protestants. The central contentious question has been the attempt by the post-independence Sudanese leaders to introduce *Sharia* laws, a move centred within Islamisation and Arabisation.[28] Islamisation and Arabisation in Sudan go back many centuries, but intensified during the 19th century slave trade. These are some of the main causes which have led to conflict in Sudan.

As we have seen, the north is dominated by Arab-speaking Sudanese—with culture, language and religion at the core of their identity. Sudan, with a rich history of Islamic nationalism (Funj sultanate, 1504-1820; and Mahdist state, 1885-1899), turned to religion as a source of strength and national image. Central to this image has been the perception by the Sudanese leaders that Islamisation performs two major objectives, namely mobilisation and identification. Though applied at variance, Islamisation still constitutes the *modus operandi* for the Sudanese administrations. The Administration of Ismail al-Azhari (1956-1958), declared "Islam the state religion and the *Sharia* a basic source of law".[29] Similarly, Gen-Ibrahim Abboud (1958-64), stressed that his policy towards the south was to be based on a "single language and a single religion for a single country".[30] The war efforts against the Anya Nya (snake poison), which were conducted until the 1972 Addis Ababa Accords were signed, were premised on this context and rationale.

In Phase One of his administration, President Gaafar al Numeiri was conciliatory and accommodating with regard to the Southern question. This is what paved the way for the Addis Ababa agreement. For the first time, the north not only recognised the Southern Sudan Liberation Movement (SSLM)—the Anya Nya political wing—as the main representative of the south, but the agreement provided for autonomy for the southern Sudanese. When he took over the leadership through a military *coup* in 1969, he was supported mainly by the left-oriented elements in Sudan, particularly the Sudan Communist Party (SCP). His *coup* was therefore dubbed a "Socialist Revolution", with an openly anti-imperialist policy stance, and support from Egypt, Libya, and the Arab countries of the Middle East.[31] Influenced by some internal developments in Sudan, Numeiri took a more radical stance *vis-à-vis* the situation in the south during Phase Two of his administration. Before dealing with Numeiri's *volte face,* it is necessary to identify the underlying causal factors.

First, the introduction of socialist policies by Numeiri's regime was opposed by the advocates of pro-Islamisation, particularly by reformers such as the Muslim Brotherhood. The followers of Muslim Brotherhood are opposed to the notion of separation of church and state, because it is not consistent with *Sharia* law and is deemed inherently destabilising. The policies were also opposed by the influential Ansar and Khatmiyya religio-political traditionalist movements, particularly their political wings, the Umma Party and the Democratic Unionist Party (DUP) respectively. Secondly, the 1971 attempted military *coup* by leftist officers influenced his decision to clamp down on SCP, his allies. Thirdly, he revoked the special status of the south which was provided for in the 1972 Addis Ababa Accords, thus distancing himself from the southerners as well. The central point to stress is that Numeiri needed a policy framework which would remove him from a political quagmire and enable him to remain at the helm of the presidency. He also needed to establish policies which were consonant with Sudan's political history and social culture, which includes the over 70% Muslim population.[32]

Numeiri therefore introduced an Islamisation policy which once again polarised the Sudanese historical political divide between the north and south. *Sharia* was incorporated in politics, law and society in general. In this case, religion—Islam—through the policy of Islamisation, was used as an instrument to unify the country and to promote the war efforts against the south, rendering his policy of "Sudanese national" identity more of a fallacy than a reality. The southern Sudanese people established the Anya

Nya II, and the Sudanese People's Liberation Army (SPLA), to liberate the people of the region from Islamisation and Arabisation policies. Under the direction of the Southern Sudan People's Liberation Movement (SSPLM) and Sudan People's Liberation Movement (SPLM), the political wings of Anya Nya II and SPLA respectively, the demand of the South henceforth focused on total liberation. Irrespective of the intra-liberation movements' conflict and the subsequent disintegration of the SSLM, the SPLA still remains the dominant military broker in the south and the major challenger to successive regimes in Khartoum. Numeiri's Islamisation policies were used as a means to promote Muslim identification and mobilisation.

Islamisation policy was introduced to conform with "a legacy left by the Mahdist movement not only of Islamic identification with the state but also of Islam's role as an anticolonialist force and an integral component of Sudanese nationalism."[33] Numeiri was originally anti-Mahdist, -Khatimiyya, and -Muslim Brothers. He stressed that Sudan was to be purified from western cultural infidelity and that backwardness in Sudan was a consequence of non-Muslim practices. Indeed, this was Numeiri's clear *volte face* if compared with his policies of the 1970s.[34] Islamisation policies solidified his authoritarian rule and legitimacy, at least initially. In this context, the state became an important instrument for the promotion of Islamisation. Specifically, Numeiri used Islamisation as a political instrument to diffuse the *elite* and students who were discontented with his policies. He also used it as a tool to mobilise the public on his side. Indeed, Islamisation was also used as a means to respond to critiques of him, such as issued from the National Front, National Islamic Front (NIF) led by Sadiq al-Mahdi, and the Muslim Brotherhood-led Islamic Charter Front Party (ICFP) of Hassan al-Turabi.

Numeiri's 1983 "Islamic Revolution" was a shift from his 1969 "Socialist revolution". Yet, his behavioural pattern reflected "Numeiri's Islam" as opposed to the envisaged "Islamic Revolution". His detractors were either sidelined or imprisoned. Institutions responsible for the implementation of *Sharia* law—"decisive justice courts" as they were called—were centralised within his office, functioning outside the framework of established state institutions. However, "the Ansar, Republican Brothers, Khatimiyya, secularists, and southern opposition leaders continued to oppose Numeiri's Islamisation program".[35]

President Numeiri was overthrown by Gen. Siwar al-Dhahad in 1985, and a year later, in 1986, elections were held. Sadiq al-Mahdi's government neither opposed nor implemented Numeiri's Islamisation programmes. He, however, emphasised that his government would implement Islamisation based on "true Islamic values".[36] Sadiq stressed that Islamisation should incorporate true Islamic values which separate modernisation from westernisation, but concurrently synthesises Islam with modern conditions. In some of his writings, Turabi, a reformist, also expressed views which were consistent with these of Sadiq. He stresses that the process of Islamisation is not static but dynamic and flexible. It is within this context, he argues, that an Islamic state must appreciate *Sharia* values and norms, and integrate them "into the Islamic framework of government".[37] Under the leadership of Hassan Ahmed Bashir who took over power through a *coup* in 1989, Islamisation as a policy framework still constitutes his government's *modus operandi*, with NIF of the Muslim Brotherhood playing an important role.[38]

These differences in the interpretation and application notwith-standing, the post-independence civilian and military leaderships in Sudan have consistently pursued the policy of Islamisation. This policy framework has persistently polarised Sudan into a dichotomised conflict between the north and south, or Muslims versus non-Muslims. The application of *Sharia* law is inherently "exclusive", with the non-Muslims viewed as incapable of holding a position of authority over Muslims.[39] The main stumbling block to *rapprochement* between the two regions is the domination associated with the imposition of Islamisation.[40] Inclusion of Islamisation in the policies in Sudan, implies that the non-Muslim areas exist in a religious and cultural vacuum. The policies of the leaderships in Sudan have therefore undermined the objective of national identity, a subject to which we will return in due course. In order to remain in leadership control, and in an effort to maintain the Sudanese national sovereignty, the regimes have spent millions of dollars to sustain one of

Sub-Saharan Africa's largest armies. Sudan spends more than $2 million a day to maintain its armed forces.

Apart from the regular Sudan People's Armed Forces (SPAF), the Government also maintains an Islamic militia called the Popular Defence Forces (PDF).[41] Table 1 clearly indicates the extent to which Sudan has mobilised and increased its armed forces and military spending in its war efforts against the liberation movements in the south, particularly since the 1980s. The escalation of conflict between the SPAF and the SPLA in the early 1980s coincided with the introduction of Islamisation policies by President Numeiri. It was during his rule that Sudan had a written Constitution for the first time. The armed forces were increased from 50 000 in 1975, to 65 000 in 1983. Excluding the PDF, the total number of the SPAF between 1992-1994, 1995-1998, and in 1999, was increased to over 80 000, 90 000 and 100 000 respectively.

Following the 1972 Addis Ababa Accords, Sudan's military expenditure reached $170 million and $150 million in 1974 and 1975 respectively. These figures increased to more than $450 million and $600 million in 1981 and 1982 respectively.

This increase in military spending coincided with the institutionalisation and politicisation of Islamisation programmes introduced a year later by Numeiri. The aim of Numeiri was to draw support from Muslims, internally and internationally, for his war efforts against the south, which by extension was to legitimise his leadership. Over the years the Sudanese civil war became increasingly internationalised, with Sudan and the liberation movements receiving material help from a number of countries.[42]

Table 6.1: Sudan: Armed forces and military expenditures 1985-1999

Year	Armed forces (thousands)	Military expenditure (US $ millions)
1985	65	146
1986	59	128
1987	59	197
1988	65	245
1989	65	280
1990	65	204
1991	65	531
1992	82	766
1993	82	304
1994	89	426
1995	90	389
1996	90	405
1997	93	413
1998	94	550
1999	110	610

Sources: US, 1995. *World Military Expenditures and Arms Transfers, 1990-1994* (Washington, D.C.: Arms Control and Disarmament Agency); and US, 2000. *World Military Expenditures and Arms Transfers, 1996-1999*, (Washington, D.C.: Arms Control and Disarmament Agency).

Table 6.1 also shows a marked increase in defence procurement by Sudan, particularly since 1989. Between 1991, 1992, and 1993, for example, Sudan's military expenditure amounted to $531 million, $766 million, and $304 million respectively. It was increased to $550 million and $610 million in 1998 and 1999 respectively. The introduction of the Islamic militia, the PDF by the leadership of Bashir, was to augment the SPAF military campaigns against the combined forces of the SPLA and the Beja Congress Armed Forces (BCAF), among others. The aim of the Sudanese government is to increase the total number of its SPAF and PDF to more than 655 000, to pursue the objective of what Bashir calls "Islamic holy" war.[43] The formation of the National Democratic Alliance (NDA), a conglomeration of Umma Party, DUP, SPLA-Mainstream, SCP, BCAF, and Sudanese Allied Forces (SAF), among others, has divided the northern ranks. The BCAF and the SAF operate along the Sudo-Eritrean and Sudo-Ethiopian borders respectively. The SPLA, however, still controls most of the south.[44] What needs to be stressed here is that since its establishment in 1995, the NDA has added a new military dimension to the Sudanese civil war. The northern opposition movements have joined hands with the SPLA to remove the NIF-led government of Bashir. This means that Muslims are fighting alongside non-Muslims against the Islamic regime of Bashir. Whereas the NDA groups of the north and the SPLA have the same objectives, the Umma Party and DUP are reluctant to renounce the idea of incorporating Islamic laws in the Constitution. What is also important is that there is a clear correlation between oil production and military spending by the Sudanese ruling *elite*. To a large extent the countries and oil companies involved in the production of oil in Sudan (see Table 6.2) are undermining conflict resolution efforts in the country.

Oil production and the Sudanese civil war

As in the case of Angola and other conflict-prone countries in Africa, mineral and oil production provide needed foreign revenue incentives for the belligerents of civil wars. In Sudan, where the debt burden accounts for 250% of the Gross Domestic Product (GDP), the production of minerals and oil by foreign private and state-owned companies provide consumption, needs and revenue earnings for the country's war efforts against the rebel movements.

Whereas Sudan consumes about 30 000 barrels per day, its production is estimated to have increased from about 12 000 in 1999, to 200 000 barrels per day in early 2000.[45] Sudan completed its 1 610 km oil pipeline, financed mainly by Talisman, connecting Heglig oilfields (Southern Darfur and Southern Kordofan) and Baishir, South of Port Sudan, as well as al-Jayli oil refinery (70 km north of Khartoum) in 1999, at a cost of $1 billion and $600 million respectively.[46] As Table 6.2 indicates, there are a number of national and international companies involved in oil production in Sudan. The companies involved in funding, building and maintaining the pipelines include, among others, Denim Pipeline Construction (Canada), Roll'n Oil Field Industries (Canada), Mannesmann (Germany), the Europipe Consortium, Weir Pumps (United Kingdom), Techint (Argentina), Allen Power Engineering (United Kingdom), and the Chinese Government. The other major oil fields include Adar (western Upper Nile) and Unity (in Bentiu area in Unity State).[47]

The oil exploration and exploitation companies operate under the auspices of the Greater Nile Petroleum Operating Company (GNPOC), a consortium of, among others, Chinese, Malaysian, Canadian, and Sudanese companies. These companies have concessions in the Adar, Heglig and Unity oilfields, all of which are located in Southern Sudan. Chevron, one of the first companies to engage in extensive petroleum production in Sudan since the 1960s, abandoned its $800 million investments due to the attacks by the SPLA. The other oil companies involved in the exploration of oil in Sudan in the 1960s and 1970s, included Agip, Texas Eastern, Sun Oil and Union Texas. After the withdrawal of Chevron from its Suakin Basin oilfields, 40 kilometres from the Red Sea, the government of Sudan signed an agreement with the Saudi Arabian businessman, Adnan Khashoggi, to establish the National Oil Company of Sudan (NOCS), to resume the production of oil in exchange for a 50% interest in the venture and related assets. Chevron sold its assets at the Abu Jarra oilfields to Concorp of Sudan, which by 1992 began the production of petroleum.[48] Sudan's oil and gas reserves are estimated at 700 million barrels, and 86 billion cubic metres (or 0,06% of the world's reserves), respectively. The oil revenue spent by the government of Sudan totals $1 million per day, equal to the amount which the government of Sudan spends on arms per day.[49]

Table 6.2:   Oil prospectors in Sudan*

Country	State/private-owned companies	Concession
Austria	OMV-GmbH	Heglig
Canada	Arakis Energy	Heglig
Canada	State Petroleum Corporation	Heglig
Canada	Talisman	Heglig
China	China National Petroleum Company	Heglig
China	Petrochina	Heglig
France	ELF-Aquitane	Heglig
France	Totalfina	Unity
Iran	National Iranian Gas Company	Unity
Italy	AGIP	Heglig
Italy	ENI	Heglig
Malaysia	Petroliam Nasional Berhad	Heglig
Mauritius	GAPCO	Heglig
Netherlands	Royal Dutch Shell	Heglig
Nigeria	Amni International Petroleum	Suakin
Qatar	Gulf Petroleum Corporation	Adar
Qatar	Gulf International	Adar
Russia	YUKOS	Adar
Russia	Zarubezh-Neftegasstroi	Adar
Saudi Arabia	Arab Group International	Heglig
Sudan	Al-Ghanawa	Melut
Sudan	CONCORP	Adar
Sudan	Sudan's National Oil Company	Heglig
Sudan	SUDAPET	Heglig
Sweden	International Petroleum Corporation	Heglig
United States	Chevron**	Unity
United States	Occidental Petroleum Corporation**	Unity
United States	Texas Eastern**	Unity
United States	Union Eastern**	Unity

*   Compiled from numerous sources including, S. Field, *The civil war in Sudan: The role of the oil industry* (Johannesburg: IGD Occasional Paper No. 23, February 2000). Some of the state and privately owned companies are engaged in the production of oil in more than one concession, that is, in the Adar, Heglig and Unity oilfields.

**   These companies have withdrawn from oil production in Sudan.

Within the GNPOC in Heglig, the Chinese state-controlled company, China National Petroleum Corporation (CNPC), owns over 40% of the shares. The CNPC, under the name of PetroChina, is also privately owned by other companies worldwide, with BP Amoco's investments alone reaching more than $576 million.[50] Whereas the Malaysian state-owned company Petroliam Nasional Berhad (Petronas) holds 30% of the shares, Talisman Energy, a Canadian private company and Sudan's state-owned company, Sudapet, hold 25% and 5% of the shares respectively.[51]

There are many other state and privately owned companies that are involved in the exploitation of petroleum. In Block 5A concession, for example, the International Petroleum Corporation (IPC) which is owned by Lundin Oil AB, a private Swedish company, owns over 40% of the shares. Petronas, OMV-GmbH of Austria, and Sudapet, own over 29%, 26% and 5% of the shares respectively. It is important to note that apart from the use of oil revenues for military procurement by Sudan, the oil exploration and exploitation companies are also concerned about security. Indeed, apart from the Sudanese soldiers and the pro-government militia deployed to protect oilfields, Chinese soldiers, mercenaries from Malaysia and Branch Heritage of the South African Executive Outcomes (EO), are also reported to be operating in the area. Executive Outcomes has links in countries in Africa, South America and the Far East, with 70% of its operations based in Africa. Whereas in Kenya the EO is reported to have established security consulting companies with Raymond Moi (Pres. Moi's son) in Sudan, the EO also provides security to the Canadian oil firm, Talisman.[52] As in the case of other interlocking conflict entanglements in Africa, the involvement of the oil-producing companies not only perpetuates the civil war, but many people have been killed and forcefully displaced from the areas surrounding the oilfields.[53]

With an estimated 12,5 billion barrels of "undiscovered" oil, Sudan is likely to be one of the world's largest oil producers. Sudan, therefore, continues to attract oil prospectors who are willing to invest in the oil industry, irrespective of the security risks involved. The marketing of Sudanese oil has recently attracted a number of competitors, with Trafigura Beheer BV of the Netherlands winning the contracts against

Vitol SA (Switzerland), Arcadia Group PLC (United Kingdom), and Glencore International AC (Switzerland).[54] As already explained, the National Islamic Front (NIF)-led government of Omar al-Bashir, or any other future regime in Khartoum for that matter, is likely to harden its position on the question of southern Sudan. An increase in the production and export of oil will not only continue to provide Sudan with the badly needed revenues for military procurement, but prospects for the establishment of a consensus on national identity will continue to be a distant dream.

It is therefore fair to argue that the countries involved in this oil exploration and exploitation, either directly or indirectly through their privately owned companies, are perpetuating the civil war and undermining the attempts by Sudan to establish a unified society based on national identity. Except for the United States whose companies have withdrawn because of the sanctions imposed by Congress, most of the countries in Europe as well as Canada, China, Russia and some third-world countries, are involved in promoting and perpetuating the forgotten tragedy in Sudan. The state and privately owned companies from China and Canada enjoy the largest share of oil production in Sudan, with the Canadian companies providing the needed technology. Some of the top executives of the oil companies have close relations with the NIF leadership. For example, the chairperson of the Board of Arakis Energy, Lutfer Khan, had close relations with the Sudanese Minister for External Security, Qutbi Mahdi. The Khan-Mahdi personal relationship paved the way for better understanding between Arakis Energy and the Sudanese government. Lutfer Khan also played an important role in encouraging Petronas to become involved in oil production in Sudan.[55] Prior to its oil prospecting and production being taken over by Talisman, Arakis was also engaged in servicing the broken SPAF trucks, as well as providing electricity and water to the army camps close to the oilfields.[56]

Islamisation and the question of "Sudanese national" identity

The 1998 new Sudanese constitution stipulates that Sudan is a unitary state in which people coexist with their cultural diversity, Islam being the religion of the majority. Christianity and other religions and doctrines are given consideration without any form of compulsion. The constitution further provides, *inter alia*, that the Islamic *Sharia*, customary law *al-urf*, and national consensus *ijma al-ummah*, constitute the basis for legislation.[57] The main issue here is the institutionalisation of religious, *Sharia* doctrines within the state apparatus. As has been explained, President Numeiri instituted separate courts to carry out judicial functions. The establishment of extra-judicial courts was done with the objective of implementing Islamisation programmes. Numeiri's Islamisation programmes contravened individual rights enshrined in the Constitution.[58] In essence, therefore, his policies were meant to promote his own political agenda and legitimacy. The courts were used to silence his critics in the name of the "violation" of Islamisation. What has been the impact of Islamisation processes on "Sudanese national" identity? The institutionalisation of Islamisation programmes, it is argued, makes "Sudan ... the only state in our age that has formally opted for Islam as its system of government".[59]

With a population of close to 30 million people, and over 500 ethnic groups speaking more than 100 languages, Sudan faces a major challenge to nation building. The decision by the leaders and Arabic-speaking Muslims to use Islam as a unifying element in the country, has met with objections in the south. Turabi, one of the influential Sudanese leaders, has emphasised that without Islam, "Sudan has no identity, no direction".[60] It is Islam, according to Turabi, which can lead Sudan to a national consensus. His view is generally in conformity with those of Sadiq who stresses that in an Islamic state like Sudan, there should be no separation of church and state, with *Sharia* protecting the rights of non-Muslims.[61] Turabi's view of an Islamic state is central to the doctrine of *tawhid* (oneness, unification, monotheism), whose function it is to carry out God's duties through *Sharia* and to act as a restraint on autocratic rule.[62] The central point to emphasise is that there are two main conflicting viewpoints which have negated the process of "Sudanese national" identity. The contradictions are centred on the dichotomy between the advocates of an Islamic state and those who are pro-secular state.

Figure 6.1 summarises the competing conceptions of a "Sudanese national" identity by the leaders of Sudan since 1956. It clearly shows consistency on the part of the administrations on the question of the institutionalisation of an Islamic state, a policy which is, however, persistently opposed by the southern movements.

Figure 6.1: A schematic model of variables inhibiting Sudanese national identity

1956-1969	Six administrations	Different political parties Military/civilian administrations Islamic state Islamisation policy Militant
1969-1985	Numeiri	SSU Islamic state Islamisation policy Moderate/militant
1985-1989	Mahdi	Umma Party/NIF Militant Islamic state Islamisation policy
1989-	Bashir	NIF Militant Islamic state Islamisation policy
1956-	Southern movements	Anya Nya I & II/Others SPLA/SPLM Militant Self-determination/secession Secular state

In the formative years of the 1950s to 1970s, the Islamic movements and more so the Islamic Charter Front—created in 1964—insisted on its advocacy for identifying the state as Islamic. In this context "the state was to be democratic and centralised", with the rights of "non-Muslims ... protected by the traditional Islamic ... roles of the people of the book *(ahl al-kitab)*".[63] This implies that Islam is a superior religion and the other religious organisations are to be protected by it. The conception is inherently exclusive and by extension inhibits conflict resolution geared towards the establishment of a "Sudanese national" identity.[64] Indeed, it was as a result of the movement towards reconciliation *(musalaha)* by Numeiri in the early 1970s, *vis-à-vis* the south, that he was vehemently opposed by those advocating Islamisation. In the same vein, Turabi stressed at the time, that as the issue of Islamisation increasingly became part and parcel of state and society, it "established a positive strategy toward the south, calling for its inclusion in the Sudanese Islamic project rather than ignoring or separating from it".[65]

For Turabi, "Sudanese national" identity was a clear reflection of his cognitive behaviouralism, practically demonstrated by his direct involvement in organising programmes in the south and supporting Muslims residing in the region. Under the leadership of Mahdi, non-Muslim regions were given the right to practice their customs and religious faiths, provided that they recognised the special place of Islam as the modal determinant of the Sudanese state.[66] For President Bashir, the issue of a federal system of government with an option of special regional autonomy for the south is being advanced, but still with Sudan viewed as an *ipso facto Islamic* state. Thus, according to this view, it is Islam which gives Sudan its *raison d'etre* as a unified entity.[67] Strictly speaking the incorporation of Islamic laws in the Sudanese constitutions since 1973 has been an attempt to legislate for religious communities and not for individuals. This policy is "virtually indistinguishable from the old Ottoman *millet* system, where *dhimmis*, or non-Muslim subjects of the Islamic state, enjoyed a measure of local autonomy according to their religious law, under what was nonetheless a clear Islamic hegemony".[68]

The Southern ethnic groups have, however, demanded (*inter alia*) a secular constitution and secular laws for Sudan, freedom of religion, as well as non-discrimination on ethnic and religious grounds. What exists in Sudan is a clash of perceptions as to "Sudanese national" identity. What we have analysed thus far in this section, requires further elaboration and focus.

I maintain that the situation in Sudan concerns two distinct and persistently competing *"isms"*. First, there exists what might be called *Arabic-speaking Sudanese nationalism*. This form of nationalism is influenced mainly by the religio-linguistic and cultural patterns which bring together Muslims in Sudan. Over 70% of the population are Muslims. It is important to note that most of the Arab-speaking Sudanese are not Arabs *per se*. They have African blood, hence their dark skin. However, it is because of Islamic faith and Arab culture and language that Arabism becomes a sense of pride and *a fortiori* unifying factor. Islam therefore functions beyond the expected boundaries of religion. It is the embodiment of the societal pillars cherished by Muslims, namely "prayer, witness, fasting, charity, and pilgrimage to Mecca; hence it embodies a complete culture which must be adopted *in toto*".[69] Apart from the dark-skinned Baggara Arabs, there are other Islamised ethnic peoples such as the Fur, Masalit, Zaghawa, the Beja, and the Arab Sudanese of the North Central. The spread of Islamic faith in Sudan occurred over centuries and was encouraged by both the Egyptians and the British.[70]

It is therefore important to stress that Islam functions as an important intervening variable which explains the consistency in Islamisation policies pursued by the civilian and military administrations in Sudan. Political power is conceptualised within this context. Islam is used to promote a religiously oriented nationalism in Sudan. It encourages a form of Islamic "ecumenicalism" (Pan-Arabism). Sudan is not only a member of the Arab League and the Organisation of Islamic Countries, but it has materially supported the Arab countries during the 1967 and 1973 Arab-Israeli wars. Sudan was also the only African country in Sub-Saharan Africa that supported Iraq in the 1991-92 Gulf War.[71] It is this Islamic theocracy which explains unity of Muslims on the one hand and division between non-Muslims and Muslims on the other—traditionally categorised as the south and north respectively. It is also the policy of Islamisation which explains the unity of the southern non-Muslims in general. For the non-Muslims, the incorporation of Islamisation implies a core-periphery relationship, a situation which is resented by the south. Control of the state apparatus thus becomes an important ingredient for group survival. "Sudanese national identity", for the Muslims, is therefore conceived in this context.

The second *"ism"* is about what might be called *African Sudanese nationalism* or better still, *secular nationalism*. This perspective embraces southern black Sudanese or non-Muslims in general. The south views the persistence of the Islamisation programme as implying that there is a religious and cultural vacuum which the north has to fill. In other words there cannot be a unified "Sudanese national" identity without Islam as the guiding religion. The south, therefore, perceives a "Sudanese national" identity within the context of *secular nationalism*, accommodating the Sudanese people irrespective of their religio-cultural values. The idea is to remove any form of religion from state apparatus. This, the south believes, would eliminate the tendency toward dominance associated with Islamisation programmes. This perspective draws our attention to the fact that a real "Sudanese national identity" must move away from policies which only "permit" other groups to exercise their religious rights, as is inherently inscribed in Islamisation. The main objective of Islamisation is to assimilate the south (non-Muslims) into an Islamic culture.

Summary and conclusion

This discussion set out to examine the issues which relate to the interplay between Islamisation and religious identification and mobilisation—and the impact of Islamisation, Arabisation and oil production on "Sudanese national identity". A number of issue areas have been clearly articulated. Firstly, the civilian and military administrations in Sudan have consistently pursued the policy of Islamisation since the independence of Sudan in 1956. Islamisation is used as a religio-political tool to promote unity in Sudan, while it is concurrently used as a means for *elite* and leadership survival by the north. It therefore becomes an important rallying point or mobilisation tool for the north *and* the south. Secondly, the policy of Islamisation hinders conflict resolution in Sudan, with the south rejecting its implied religious and political superiority and domination. Third, the involvement of state and privately owned oil companies in Sudan continues to hamper progress towards reaching a consensus on national identity. As we have indicated, oil production also plays a negative role in conflict resolution in Sudan.

The divergent perspectives of the north and south have prevented the meaningful establishment of a "Sudanese national identity". Whereas the north and south accept the politically based entity called "Sudan", and that it is only through "unity in diversity" that "Sudan" can remain a unified whole, they still differ on the process and modalities which can lead to its achievement. Thus the south has persistently rejected the policy of Islamisation because it is exclusionary and inherently discriminatory. Pursuit of the policy of Islamisation, whether formally institutionalised or otherwise, therefore defeats the purpose of "Sudanese national" identity. The policy is a fallacy in that it renders the process of unity of the north and the south nugatory. It is important to stress that Sudan has failed to achieve the objective of "national identity", not because of group identification *per se*, but through how the "national identity" framework is defined, and therefore the impact it has on the different groups in the country.[72] As I have explained, the core of the problem, which negates the Sudanese "national identity", is found in the Islamisation programmes pursued by the civilian and military administrations. Islamic identity is "the problem", with the south resisting religio-cultural assimilation and its corollary, racial discrimination. I have also explained that the south does not simply reject a unified Sudan as such, but rather the political domination inherent in the transformation of Sudan into an Islamic state. As a means for the control of economic resources and political power, the state, therefore, has become the centre of contestation between the south and the north, leading to what has been called a "zero-sum confrontation".[73]

Notes and References

[1]   Korwa G. Adar, "Sudan: The Internal and External Contexts of Conflict and Conflict Resolution", *The United Nations High Commissioner for Refugees, Writenet, forthcoming*; and generally Korwa G. Adar, "Islamisation in Sudan: The Fallacy of the Sudanese Administrations' Policy of National Identity", in Pietro Toggia, Patrick Lauderdale, and Abebe Zegeye (eds), *Terror and Crisis in the Horn of Africa: Autopsy of Democracy, Human Rights and Freedom* (Aldershot: Ashgate, 2000). 209-228 and Korwa G. Adar, 2000. "New Regionalism and Conflict Resolution: The Case of the Intergovernmental Authority on Development in Sudan", in *African Journal on Conflict Resolution* Vol. 1, No. 2. pp. 39-66.

[2]   Ali A. Mazrui and Michael Tidy, 1984. *Nationalism and New States in Africa.* Nairobi: Heinemann, p. 194. See also generally, E. O'Ballance, 1977. *The Secret War in the Sudan, 1955-1972.* London: Faber and Faber; P.M. Holt, 1961. *A Modern History of the Sudan.* London: Weidenfield and Nicolson; and I. Ewald, 1990. *Soldiers, Traders and Slaves: State Formation and Economic Transformation in the Greater Nile Valley, 1700-1885.* Madison: University of Wisconsin Press.

[3]   See D.M. Wai, 1973. "The Southern Sudan: The Country and the People", in D.M. Wai (Ed.), *The Southern Sudan: The Problem of National Integration.* London: Frank Cass. p. 3.

[4]   See generally, Mohamed Omer Beshir, 1968. *The Southern Sudan: Background to Conflict.* London: Hurst and Co; I. O'Brian, 1993. "Ethnicity, National Identity and Social Conflict", in A. Hurskainen and M. Salih (eds). *Social Science and Conflict Analysis.* Uppsala: Helsinki University Press; C. Eprile, 1972. *Sudan: The Long War.* London: Institute for the Study of Conflict; I. Oduho and W. Deng, 1963. *The Problem of the Southern Sudan.* London: Oxford University Press; and G. Warburg, 1978. *Islam, Nationalism and Communism in a Traditional Society: The Case of Sudan.* London: Frank Cass.

[5]   Korwa G. Adar, 2000. "Secularism and Islamism in Sudan: Contesting the National Consensus", in *South African Yearbook of International Affairs, 2000/01* Johannesburg: The South African Institute of International Affairs. pp. 301-315.

[6] B. Malwal, 1981. *People and Power in Sudan—the Struggle for National Stability.* London: Ithaca Press.

[7] A.M. Lesch, 1998. *The Sudan-Contested National Identities.* Oxford: James Currey, p. 21 and generally, M. Mahmoud, 1997, "Sufism and Islamism in the Sudan", in D. Westerlund and E.E. Rosender (eds). *African Islam and Islam in Africa.* Athens: Ohio University Press. pp. 162-192.

[8] John, L. Esposito, 1991. *Islam: The Straight Path.* Oxford: Oxford University Press. p. 211.

[9] Ibid. See also Najm A. Bezirgan, "Islam and Arab Nationalism", in *Middle East Review*, Vol. 11, No. 2 (Winter 1978-79). pp. 38-44l; and Carl Leiden, "Arab Nationalism Today", in *Middle East Review* Vol. 11, No. 2. (Winter 1978-79). pp. 45-51.

[10] John L. Esposito, 1991. *Islam and Politics.* 3rd ed. New York: Syracuse University Press. p. 34.

[11] John Obert Voll, 1982. *Islam: Continuity and Change in the Modern World.* Boulder CO: Westview Press. p. 246.

[12] Ibid. p. 137.

[13] James P. Piscatori, 1994. *Islam in a World of Nation-States.* Cambridge: Cambridge University Press. For a detailed analysis of this viewpoint in relation to Sudan, see John L. Esposito and John O. Voll, 1996. *Islam and Democracy.* Oxford: Oxford University Press; Nazib Ayubi, 1993. *Political Islam: Religion and Politics in the Arab World.* New York: Routledge; Alexander S. Cudsi, 1989. "Islam and Politics in Sudan", in James P. Piscatori (Ed.). *Islam in the Political Process.* Cambridge: Cambridge University Press. pp. 36-55; and Milton Viorst, 1995. "Sudan's Islamic Experiment", in *Foreign Affairs*, Vol. 74, No. 3. (May/June). pp. 45-58.

[14] See generally, N.J. Coulson, 1957. "The State and the Individual in Islamic Law", *International and Comparative Law Quarterly.* pp. 49-60; and Ann K.S. Lambton, 1981. *State and Government in Medieval Islam: An Introduction to the Study of Islamic Political Theory: The Jurists.* Oxford: Oxford University Press.

[15] Lambton, *State and Government in Medieval Islam.* p. xvi.

[16] Esposito and Volli, *Islam and Democracy.* p. 41.

[17] See, for example, Suzanne Haneef, 1982. *What Everyone Should Know About Islam and Muslims.* Chicago: Kazi Publications; and Arthur Goldschmidt, 1988. *A Concise History of the Middle East.* 3rd ed. Boulder: Westview Press.

[18] For a detailed treatment of Islamisation and democratisation, see Esposito and Volli, *Islam and Democracy.* pp. 1-32; and Jacob Landan,1990. *The Politics of Pan-Islam: Ideology and Organization.* Oxford: Clarendon Press.

[19] Ann E. Mayer, 1991. *Islam and Human Rights: Tradition and Politics.* Boulder CO: Westview. pp. 143-161. See also generally, Rudolph Peters, 1979. *Islam and Colonialism: The Doctrine of Jihad and Modern History.* The Hague: Mouton; and John Kelsay (ed.). 1993. *Just War and Jihad: War, Peace, and Statecraft in the Western and Islamic Traditions.* Westport, Conn: Greenwood Press.

[20] Lambton, *State and Government in Medieval Islam,* p. 205

[21] Mayer, *Islam and Human Rights,* p. 148. See also Joseph Schacht, 1964. *Introduction to Islamic Law.* Oxford: Clarendon Press. pp. 130-31.

[22] Sultanhussein Tabandeh, (Transl. F.J. Goulding), 1970. *A Muslim Commentary on the Universal Declaration of Human Rights.* Guildford: F.J. Goulding, 1970. p. 18.

[23] Ibid. p. 17

[24] Mayer, *Islam and Human Rights.* p. 152.

[25] Esposito, *Islam: The Straight Path.* p. 210. See also, John Esposito, 1991. *Islam and Politics,* 3rd edition.. New York: Syracuse University Press. pp. 293-293.

[26] For a detailed historical evolution of the "Southern Problem", see for example, Beshir, *The Southern Sudan;* Fristram Betts, 1974. *The Southern Sudan: The Ceasefire and After.* London: The Africa Publications Trust; Othwonk Dak, (n.d.) *Southern Sudan: The Internationalisation of the Problem.* Khartoum: E.C. Gurashi; Abdelwahab el-Affendi, 1991. *Turabi's Revolution: Islam and Power in the Sudan.* London: MacMillan; Yusuf Fadl Hasan, 1967. *The Arabs and the Sudan from the Seventh to the Early Sixteenth Century.* Edinburgh:

Edinburgh University Press; and R.O. Collins, 1971. *Land Beyond the Rivers: The Southern Sudan 1898-1918.* Cambridge: Yale University Press.

27 John Howell, 1973. "Politics in the Southern Sudan", in *African Affairs,* Vol. 72 (287), (April). pp. 163-178. See also, R.K. Badal, 1976. "The Rise and Fall of Separatism in Southern Sudan", in *African Affairs,* Vol. 75(301), (October). pp. 463-474.

28 See generally, Muddathir Abd Al-Rahim, 1970. "Arabism, Africanism, and Self Identification in the Sudan", in *Journal of Modern African Studies*, Vol. 8, No. 2. pp. 233-249; and Oluwadare Aguda, 1973. "Arabism and Pan-Arabism in Sudanese Politics", *Journal of Modern African Studies*, Vol. 11, No. 2. pp. 177-200.

29 Esposito, *Islam and Politics,* p. 231. Prior to the 1969 *coup,* the six Sudanese Administrations of al-Azhari (1956-58), Gen. Ibrahim Abboud (1958-64), Sayed Sir el-Khatim el-Khalifa (1964-65), Muhammad Ahmed Mahgoub (1965-66), Sadiq al-Mahdi (1966-67), and Muhamad Ahmed Mahgoub (1967-69)—used religion (Islam) as the guiding principle of their policies *vis-à-vis* the south.

30 Assefa, *Mediation of the Civil Wars.* p. 58.

31 M. Khalid, 1985. *Numeiri and the Revolution of Dismay.* London: KPI Publishers.

32 See generally, John L. Esposito, 1991. *Islam and Politics,* 3rd ed. New York: Syracuse University Press; John O. Voll, 1984. *Political Impact of Islam in the Sudan.* Washington, D.C.: U.S. Department of State; John L. Esposito, 1986. "Sudan's Islamic Experiment", in *Muslim World*, Vol. 76 (July/October). pp. 181-201; and Bona Malwal, 1985. *The Sudan: A Second Challenge to Nationhood.* New York: Thornton Books.

33 Esposito, *Islam and Politics.* p. 231; and generally, Ann M. Lesch, 1987. "A View From Khartoum", in *Foreign Affairs* (Spring). pp. 807-826.

34 Assefa, *Mediation of the Civil Wars.* p. 72.

35 Esposito, *Islam and Politics.* pp. 237-238.

[36] Peter Bechtold, 1991. "The Sudan Since the Fall of Numayri", in Robert O. Freedman (ed.). *The Middle East from the Iran-Contra to the Intifada.* New York: Syracuse University Press. p. 24.

[37] Hassan al-Turabi,1983. "The Islamic State", in John L. Espisoto (Ed.), *Voices of Resurgent Islam.* New York: Oxford University Press. pp. 249-250; and generally, El-Affendi, *Turabi's Revolution*

[38] Ann M. Lesch,1989. "Khartum Diary", in *Middle East Report,* Vol. 161 (November-December). p. 37. See also generally, John O. Voll, 1990. "Political Crisis in the Sudan", in *Current History,* Vol. 89(546) (April). pp. 169-187.

[39] For a different perspective, see Abdullahi Ahmed An-Naim, 1989. "Constitutionalism and Islamisation in the Sudan", in *Africa Today,* Vol. 36 No. 3/4. pp. 11-28.

[40] On this point, see generally Francis Deng, 1994. "The Sudan: Stop the Carnage", in *Brookings Review,* Vol. 12, No.1, (Winter 1994). pp. 6-11; and Omar al-Nagar, 1997. The Sudan, Forging an Identity? The State and Identity in Conflict. Paper presented at the *Conference on Identity and Conflict in Africa,* African Studies Unit, University of Leeds, 15th-17th September 1997.

[41] US Government, March 1996. *Sudan Human Rights Practices, 1995.* Washington, D.C.: US Deparment of State. p. 1

[42] For a detailed analysis of the internationalisation of the civil war in Sudan see, Korwa G. Adar, 1998. "A State Under Siege: The Internationalisation of the Sudanese Civil War", in *African Security Review,* Vol. 7, No.1. pp. 44-53.

[43] "Sudan: Government Says 655,000 to Join Army", in *Horn of Africa Bulletin.* Vol. 10, No. 2 (March-April 1998). p. 27.

[44] See "Sudan/Egypt: Calling the Shots After Addis Ababa", in *African Confidential.* Vol. 36, No.14. (7 July 1995). pp.1-4.

[45] *Horn of Africa Bulletin*, 2000. "Oil Exports Rise" 12(2)(March-April), p. 35.

[46] Field, February 2000. *The Civil War in Sudan: The Role of the Oil Industry.* Johannesburg: Institute for Global Dialogue. p. 6.

[47] *Company News Africa*, 1998 (3 April). "Sudan Signs Pipeline Contract with British, Chinese and Argentinian Firms".

[48] *New Africa*, 2000. "Sudan Mining Sector". (Internet: http//www.newafrica.com/mining/sudan.htm) (Accessed 17 July).

[49] *Mbendi Information for Africa, 1995-2000*, 2000. "Oil Industry Profile-Upstream Sudan" (Internet: http//www.mbendi.co.za/indu/oilg/oilgsuus.htm). (Accessed 24 June).

[50] Ibid

[51] South Sudanese Friends International, 2000. *Oil in Sudan*. Bloomington, IN. 14 June. (Internet: http//www.geocities.com/ssfi/issues/oil000614). (Accessed 17 July).

[52] K.A. O'Brien, 1998. "Military-Advisory Groups and African Security: Privatised Peacekeeping?", *International Peacekeeping*. Vol. 5, No. 3 (Autumn). pp. 78-105.

[53] Canada, Department of International Affairs and International Trade, *Human Security in Sudan: The Report of a Canadian Assessment Mission Prepared for the Minister for Foreign Affairs*. Ottawa: January (Internet: http//www-dfait-maeci.ac.ca/foreignp/menu-e.asp). (Accessed 23 June).

[54] *Dow Jones Business News*, 1999. "Dutch-Based Trafigura Reportedly Wins Sudan Oil-Marketing Deal", 2 August.

[55] Field, The Civil War in Sudan. p. 12.

[56] R. Chatterjee, 1997. "Canada-Sudan: Activists Condemn Oil Company's Operations in Sudan", *Inter Press Service*, 26 August.

[57] See generally, SUDAN, 1998. *Constitution of the Republic of Sudan*. Khartoum: Government Printing Office; and "Sudan Endorses Draft Constitution" in *Horn of Africa Bulletin*, Vol.10, No. 2, (March-April 1998). pp. 25-26.

[58] Mayer, *Islam and Human Rights*. pp. 38-39.

[59] Milton Viorst, 1995. "Sudan's Islamic Experiment", in *Foreign Affairs*, Vol. 74, No. 3, (May/June). p. 45.

[60] Ibid., p. 46.

[61] Gabriel Warburg, 1995. "Mahdism and Islamism in Sudan", in *International Journal of Middle East Studies,* Vol. 27. pp. 219-236.

[62] Al-Turabi, "The Islamic State", in Esposito, (Ed.) *Voices of Resurgent Islam.* pp. 241-244; Al-Turabi, 1993. "The Islamic Awakening's New Wave", in *New Perspective Quarterly,* Vol. 10, No. 3 (Summer), p. 43; and Jane Perlez, "A Fundamentalist Finds a Fulcrum in Sudan", *The New York Times,* 29 January 1992.

[63] Esposito and Voll, *Islam and Democracy,* p. 96; See also generally, Muhammad Asad, 1963. *Islam and Politics.* Geneva: Islamic Centre.

[64] Esposito and Voll, *Islam and Democracy.* p. 97.

[65] Ibid. and generally, Turabi, "The Islamic State", in Esposito (ed.). *Voices of Resurgent Islam.*

[66] Francis Deng and Prosser Gifford, 1987. *The Search for Peace and Unity in the Sudan.* Washington, D.C.: The Wilson Centre Press.

[67] See Ayubi, *Political Islam.* pp. 104-113; Cudsi, "Islam and Politics in Sudan", in Piscatori (Ed.), *Islam in the Political Process.* pp. 36-55l; and Mervyn Hiskett, 1994. *The Course of Islam in Africa.* Edinburgh: Edinburgh University Press. Chapter 3.

[68] Hiskett, *The Course of Islam in Africa,* p. 90. See also Affendi, *Turabi's Revolution.* pp. 170-183.

[69] See Abd al-Rahim, "Arabism, Africanism, and Self-Identification". p. 244l; and generally, Aguda, "Arabism and Pan-Africanism in Sudanese Politics"; Bezirgan, "Islam and Arab Nationalism"; and Leiden, "Arab Nationalism Today".

[70] For a detailed analysis of the development of Islamic faith in Sudan, see Mohamed Omer Beshir, 1969. *Educational Development in the Sudan, 1985-1956.* Oxford: Oxford University Press; and Yousif Fodl Hassan, 1967. *The Arabs and the Sudanese.* Edinburgh: Edinburgh University Press.

[71] Adar, "A State Under Siege". p. 46.

[72] Francis M. Deng, et al. 1996. *Sovereignty as Responsibility: Conflict Management in Africa.* Washington, D. C.: Brookings Institution. p. 87.

[73] Ibid. p. 89.

Chapter 7

Intercultural Identity Structure of Second Generation French Women of African Descent

Vijé Franchi and Anne Andronikof-Sanglade

The ... hybrid is not only double-voiced and double-accented ... but is also double-languaged; for in it there are not only (and not even so much) two individual consciousnesses, two voices, two accents, as there are [doubling of] socio-linguistic, consciousnesses, two epochs ... that come together and consciously fight it out on the territory of the utterance ... It is the collision between differing points of view on the world that are embedded in these forms ... such unconscious hybrids have been at the same time profoundly productive historically: they are pregnant with potential for new world views, with new "internal forms" for perceiving the world in words.[1]

(Bakhtin, 1981:360)

How does one speak of women in African immigrant communities in Paris, women of all ages and of different generations, without betraying the uniqueness of each age, the singularity of each generation? Moreover, how does one explore the structuring of identity among young women raised in these so-called "communities", when the very notion of African immigrant communities can obscure the distinctions to be drawn between Diaspora communities and those found in the native African country?

This chapter advocates a clear distinction between the issues facing migrant women, or women of the first generation, from those facing French-born young women of the second generation. The experiences and challenges facing these two distinct generations cannot be conflated by

115

assuming their concurrence within the confines of imagined spatial and temporal locations in the Diaspora.

In the case of first generation migrants from Africa to France, the difficulties tackled by most migrants, including language inadequacies, a general unfamiliarity with the expectations and customs of the host country (what anthropologists refer to as cultural discontinuities)[2], are compounded by a relationship with France that is conditioned by a long history of colonisation, racial oppression and unequal access to power. Furthermore, for many of these women, immigrating to France is not a choice to which they necessarily have the right to freely consent. Rather, their inferior and oppressed status as women obliges them to follow their husbands to the new and often alienating Diaspora context. This separates them from family and community and leaves them unprotected in the face of further oppression and domination at the hands of their husbands and relatives in these so-called immigrant communities in France. In the home country, the wife's father, brothers, family and community constitute an important psychological and emotional resource and recourse for her in the case of the man abusing his power as a husband. However, in the Diaspora context, she is often isolated from all resources and recourse, a predicament that is compounded by the absence of controls or sanctions on the behaviour of the men that surround her. The psychological and material threat of being sent back to the home country without her children is a further restraining mechanism against any envisaged departure from her assigned role and identity as a wife.

Nonetheless, despite these highly constraining factors, of which the above enumeration is but a short list of examples, women of the first generation exhibit remarkable courage and inventiveness. This is evident in the way they shape their relationship to their African culture and to their predicament as women, wives, and mothers in a foreign country. It seems a distinguishing characteristic of both 1st and 2nd generation women that they possess a particular distance and perspective on culture. This mediates the way they relate to the gender constraints of their African culture of origin, the discrimination and inferior status assigned to them by the new French host culture, and the tensions and conflicts engendered by contact between these two very different cultures of unequal status.

In the case of the 1st generation, this particular perspective is a function of what Suàrez-Orozco and Suàrez-Orozco (1995)[3] have called *"the immigrant's dual frame of reference"*. It consists of the ability to view and experience their present predicament not in terms of the ideals and expectations of French society, but rather from the viewpoint of the ideals and expectations of the "old culture" (De Vos, 1973).[4] Central to such an orientation is the belief that their current lot is an improvement on what they had or could hope to have in the home country.

For many of these African immigrant women this idea of improvement is projected onto their children. For them, their lot may seem considerably aggravated by migration to a new country. However, the prospect of numerous gains for their children (better schooling and opportunities in the future), seem to buffer them against many an adversity experienced in migrating and settling in an often hostile homogenising and discriminating, dominant host society.

This chapter argues that the rose-tinted lens of a dual frame of reference applies equally to the way these women perceive and experience their relationship with the African culture of origin. This excludes the obvious acculturation effects engendered by contact and "contamination" between cultures. The migration of a culture from its native context implies selection and manipulation of its codes and patterns, informed by factors contingent upon, amongst other things, the individual's subjective reasons for migrating (which in the case of many of these women is less a matter of choice than of obligation). In the case of migrant African women, we argue that it is this dual frame of reference that permits them to consider the culture of origin in the light of the new Diaspora context. They then select and modify those aspects of it which are to be transplanted to the pockets of immigrant communities scattered across the Eastern shoulder of Paris. Ironically, Eliot (1949) described this very phenomenon with regard to migrating colonising cultures: "The people have taken with them only a part of the total culture".[5]

It could be argued that the manner in which these women deliberately prioritise, migrate and transplant specific aspects of their culture in France, attests not only to this dual frame of reference, but also to a measure of autonomy and agency. These are perhaps a function of stepping out of the mould of one's home culture, community and country, into an intercultural space of cultural plurality, inequity and difference, of collisions between differing world views and ways of constructing identity.

The modified African culture is partial—it is an immigrant or migration culture. In one sense it is crystallised, flawless and preserved, shimmering and frozen; bearing both an uncanny resemblance and a striking difference from the parent culture. The women's authorship of this partial immigrant culture permits them subsequently to exercise a measure of autonomy in regard to the constraints imposed on them as African women, and to begin to contest the gendered role assigned to them in their communities of origin. This appears to be the flip-side of the double jeopardy of their predicament as immigrant African women in a deregulated Diaspora context; it is a space in which to begin to question and contest, if not to radically change. Examples of radical contestation or transformation of these monoculturally referenced African gendered identities, are to be found less amongst this first generation than amongst their daughters.

Born in France, the 2nd generation can lay claim to more than a dual frame of reference: they bear witness to dual cultural affiliations, dual nationality, and intercultural embeddedness of their subjective experience, personal histories and identities. They are examples of Bakhtin's (1981) "hybrid forms", "pregnant with potential for new world views", with new "internal forms" for perceiving the world ... It is in articulation with their dialogic consciousness and experience of culture that they construct a representation of themselves at the personal and cultural levels.

Dual frame of reference, in the case of this 2nd generation, implies a process of socialisation characterised by dual or doubled enculturation. Moreover, it is underpinned by an intimate understanding of both cultures' partial, relative but unequal status in the intercultural context. The 2nd generation is born to and displays agency with regard not only to "partial" immigrant and host cultures, but also to those "*in-betweens*" of culture that

Bhabha (1996) describes as "*the contaminated yet connective tissue between cultures—at once the impossibility of culture's containedness and the boundary between. [...]*"[6] Their understanding and agency extends to the counterpart of the intercultural space they inhabit: namely, that partial "host" culture that, like the immigrant culture, is an unsigned forgery of "authentic" French culture. It is that aspect of French culture that is presented to those designated by the dominant as its "false nationals" or "2nd generation immigrants".

A large part of dominant French culture remains invisible and inaccessible to immigrants. However, though excluded from this "true national French culture", youths of African immigrant backgrounds, or France's new "false nationals" paradoxically and inadvertently underwrite the "authenticity" of this culture by the politically orchestrated visibility and indeterminacy of a "false national culture" of which they are designated to be the carriers. Activated by what Etienne Balibar (1990) calls the identificatory language of discrimination working in reverse, this is a process whereby "the racial/cultural identity of 'true nationals' remains invisible but is inferred from ... the quasi-hallucinatory visibility of the 'false nationals' ..."[7] Though born in France, these young women of African immigrant descent are denied access to "authentic" (white, Christian, male) French national culture, as well as to an identity as "true nationals". Rather, their assigned political identity as 2nd generation migrants underscores their difference from "true nationals" and their affiliation to "another", and in their case racially prejudiced, colonised, culture. Moreover, as we have argued, it simultaneously reinforces the authenticity of the culture and the identity to whose margins they are banished.

This discussion, however, brings a new dimension to bear on the picture. We argue, based on empirical findings, that these youths interrupt and challenge the homogenous claims of democratic French society. They bear witness not only to the displaced and disjunctive present of transplanted migratory African culture, but also to both the discriminatory and homogenising penchant of the dominant French host culture, and to the unequal footing of the two cultures at their points of interface (or clash) in the intercultural domain. We propose that their peculiar vision and perspective on culture is a function of their embeddedness in an intercultural life context. Hence, their experience and understanding of the racially and culturally inequitable mélange of "part" or "partial" cultures that charac-terise this context, and of the intercultural tensions amongst and in articulation with which they construct their identities. It is from this standpoint that we argue that these youths exhibit autonomous agency and cultural expertise in structuring their identities. They avail themselves not only of their privileged understanding of each of their reference cultures, but also of the nature of the contact between them, as they strategically recruit from the intersections of these "part cultures in contact" the stuff from which to structure their gendered intercultural identities.

In their research with US-born second generation Latino youths, Suàrez-Orozco and Suàrez-Orozco (1996) argue that one should be less concerned with the place where the individual was born and rather focus on their subjective identification (e.g., as Mexican, Chicano, Latino, Salvadoran, etc.). These authors refer to individuals born in the host country, but whose cultural identity is referenced only in relation to their country of origin (e.g. Mexicans or Salvadoran and not Mexican-Americans) as "intergenerational" Latinos, thereby placing them in a metaphorical no-man's land or in a suspended corridor between generations. The present chapter offers a very different model from the one cited above. It postulates that the French-born generation differs from the migrant generation primarily by virtue of their doubled or hybrid cultural consciousness of culture, a dual process of self-referencing identity and an embeddedness of the self in the intercultural context created by the contact between two part cultures in contact.

Moreover, this chapter takes a critical view of the previous trend, inherited from anthropology, to study the "ethnic identity" of youths of African immigrant descent. It argues that the construct of "ethnic identity" is reductive and displacing: it reduces the identity dynamics of "hybrid" youths to the simple reproduction and reification of gendered African identities within a displaced Diaspora context. We argue that any endeavours to remand young nationals of immigrant descent to an "unmarked, authentic 'African' origin or pre-text", by uncritically attempting to study their minority ethnic identity, could banish critical information from consciousness. These memories are about the construction of identity in articulation with the very discriminatory attributions (second generation immigrant; African; Arab) that underscore the exclusion of these youths from any and all claims to a "true" or "authentic" national identity. The "ethnic identity" approach distorts our understanding of the dual cultural affiliation of these youths and of their "hybrid" consciousness of culture. It obscures the intercultural embeddedness of their identities and overshadows the cultural tensions which mark the ill-defined boundaries between their "partial" reference cultures, by imagining them to be hermetic, substantive and homogenous, and "identity" to be referenced solely in relation to the "mono"culture of the parents.

This discussion endeavours to problematise the phenomena underlying the structuring of identities among young women belonging to this highly problematised second or hybrid generation of French-born youths of African immigrant descent. We analyse the cultural self-representations of French-born young females of different African backgrounds through the lens of the two phenomena that we have addressed above. These are the experience and structure or form of identity among youths of immigrant descent: namely, their *intercultural* embeddedness, and the *agency* with which national, racial, ethnic and religious identity markers are recruited and structured from the intersections of cultures, both partial and indeterminate.

The intercultural nature of the context refers to the tensions created by contact between partial African immigrant and French host cultures, whose differing values, systems of meaning and world views converge to produce conflicting and competing conceptions of personhood. For this first, French-born generation of youth raised in an African immigrant family and schooled in the host culture, the intercultural nature of the identity context frames the identity processes. These are activated during the years of junior and senior high school, and further complicate the negotiation of personally meaningful and socially valued identities.

Raised as they are in the midst of interfacing immigrant and French communities, their cultural affiliations are doubled, as are their construal of identity, their system of values, their consciousness and their language. All these factors come together and fight it out on the intercultural terrain of the structuring of their representation of "self". According to Camilleri (1990, 1994),[8] when presented with conflicting cultural codes in contact, youths respond by developing "identity strategies" that permit them to strategically manoeuvre between the opposing camps to which they belong, simultaneously appeasing each culture's identity demands, while safeguarding personally meaningful definitions of self.

The phenomenon of *agency* underscores the way in which they locate their identities in the space mapped out by the contact between these conflicting conceptions of personhood. Each dimension proposes a particular national, racial, regional, religious and ethnic profile which the youth is expected to embody as a member of that culture. Preliminary findings of a study of identity among French-born female youths of different African immigrant backgrounds point to the fact that these youths structure their representations of themselves interculturally. In other words, they enlist national, ethnic, racial, regional, and religious identity markers from both of their reference cultures and structure them into different combinations. This structurally intercultural identity contrasts sharply with the identity attributions made by significant others, whether African immigrant or French, whose construals of the "hybrid" youth are always framed in monocultural terms, as either belonging to or different from their own particular "authentic", homogenous culture.

The central thesis of this chapter is that by defining themselves in intercultural terms, these youths contest the narrow subject locations mapped out for them by significant others. They perceive themselves not as members of one or the other monocultures, but as both affiliated and excluded from each of these "partial" cultures. Their self-representations speak of their subjective *intercultural* experience of identity, and of their capacity to shift between monocultural sites of identity, strategically inhabiting their intercultural in-betweens. However, at no time should the agency that they exhibit in structuring their identities be seen to negate the deleterious effects of negative stereotyping and constraining identity attributions.[9] Rather, the structuring of their representations of themselves, interculturally, should be seen as a strategy for contesting the circumscribed locations of assigned identities and exercising authorship in the creation of new intercultural locations from which to be and act their "hybrid" consciousness of themselves and their context, in spite of considerable pressures to embody prescribed and inferior gendered cultural identities.

The study

A study undertaken in 1997 compared the structure and content of the self-concepts and cultural representations of self among 850 youths of differing cultural backgrounds. We hypothesised that the recruitment and structuring of different dimensions of the *self-concept* (physical, intrapersonal, interpersonal, school, extracurricular, and cultural) and of the *intercultural representations of self* (French nationality, immigrant nationality, ethnicity, race, and religion) would vary differentially. This variance could be attributed to the youth's gender, cultural background, level of schooling, plans to stay in France after completing school, and his/her parents' plans to return to their country of origin.

The data presented below are taken from 478 of the original 690 French-born youths. The sample comprises 246 females and 232 males, divided into three groups according to their particular African immigrant backgrounds, namely, West, Central and East African immigrant (N=164); North African (Tunisian, Moroccan and Algerian) immigrant (N=274), and mixed African immigrant and French (N=40) origins. The preliminary results of this part of the study yielded three sets of findings that bear directly on the present discussion:

Firstly, the results indicated that all French-born youths of African immigrant backgrounds recruit and structure their cultural self-attributions (national, ethnic, religious, regional and racial identity markers) interculturally. They do this by enlisting cultural identity markers from each of their reference cultures into their representations of themselves, and structuring them using one of six different combinations or patterns. These six intercultural structures were identified using a grounded-theory approach, which saturated all 850 of the original coded responses.

Table 7.1: Six structures of intercultural representations of the self

1)	*Dual* French-immigrant nationality
2)	*French* only
3)	*Immigrant nationality* only
4)	*Ethnicity* and (immigrant nationality/religion)
5)	*Race* and (immigrant nationality/ethnicity/religion)
6)	*French* and (immigrant nationality/race/ethnicity/religion)

Secondly, we found that unlike the content domains used in their self-concepts, which varied primarily with gender and level of schooling, in the case of their cultural representation of themselves, the six intercultural structures varied only according to the youth's cultural background. Both the type (national, regional, ethnic, religious or racial) of identity markers chosen, and the ways in which they were combined (to yield one of the six possible structures), depended exclusively on their geographical origin of immigration. The two distinguishing contrasts were whether the young females were of North African (Algeria, Morocco or Tunisia), West, Central and East African or mixed French and African immigrant origin.

In the North African immigrant group, over two-thirds (73%) of the young females used *North African nationality* as the central marker in their representations of themselves. Of this 73%, 20% also defined themselves in terms of race, and 15% said that they were of dual nationality.

The young females in the West, Central and East African group prioritised *ethnicity* more than any other group of youths of African descent. Over half of this group defined themselves in terms of their African ethnicity, and of these, 30% also defined themselves in terms of their African nationality and religion and 16% in terms of their race. Only 10% said that they were of dual French-African nationality, in addition to citing their ethnicity, race and religion. Of the third of the group who did not make mention of ethnicity, all defined themselves exclusively in terms of their African nationalities.

Table 7.2: Cross-cultural variation in use of intercultural structures (%)

Intercultural structures	Female and male subjects of different African origins					
	East African female	Female	African female	East African male	Male	African male
Dual French/immigrant nationality	8,16	14,48	25,00	6,06	17,12	50,00
French only	1,02	3,12	25,00	3,03	2,05	15,00
Immigrant nationality only	34,69	50,00	20,00	33,33	47,26	15,00
Ethnicity and (immigrant nationality/religion)	29,59	7,03	5,00	22,72	5,47	5,00
Race and (immigramt nationality/ethnicity)	16,32	19,53	5,00	28,78	25,34	15,00
Church and (nationality/race/ethnicity/religion)	10,20	5,46	20,00	6,06	2,73	0,00
Total	(98)=100	(128)=100	(20)=100	(66)=100	(146)=100	(20)=100

In the third group of mixed French and African immigrant parents, over two-thirds (70%) prioritised their *French nationality* in presenting their cultural representation of themselves. Of these, a quarter described themselves only in terms of French nationality, while a quarter defined themselves as dual French-African nationals. Twenty percent (20%) of the female youths who said they were of dual nationality, also defined themselves in terms of race, ethnicity and religion. As was the case in the above two groups, those members of this group who did not mention French nationality (20%), all defined themselves exclusively in terms of their African nationality.

The third finding is an extrapolation of the data presented above. These results indicate that the structures used in the cultural representations of self vary with the youths' cultural backgrounds, in ways that clearly reflect the combined identity concerns of both their reference cultures. The findings lead us to suppose that youths of different immigrant backgrounds prioritise different types of identity markers in their representations of themselves, depending on the type of markers that are flagged for both positive and negative cultural identification by each of their reference groups. For instance, interestingly, the only cultural marker recruited from the French "part" culture was nationality, in contrast to the defining characteristics of ethnicity, race, religion and nationality which were recruited from the African culture or country of origin.

This could be explained by the fact that while nationality is more defining of one's civil status in France than any ethnic, religious, or regional identities, this is certainly not the case for the African community of origin. One could argue that different states or regions in Africa prioritise different identities, ones that reflect the history and imperatives of that particular geographical and political location. For instance, the young females of North African descent prioritised their national identities in defining themselves culturally, thereby reflecting the political and historical concerns of their Algerian, Moroccan or Tunisian parents. In the same way, ethnicity, which was central to their peers of West African descent, cuts across historically constructed geographic and national borders and is often construed by their parents to be the determining indicator for cultural identity.

However, in both of the above groups, young females structured these markers in intercultural terms, recruiting from across the cultural divide in ways that clearly echo and convey the young women's experiences of belonging to two part cultures in contact. There were also indications of being raised at the interface of differing conceptions of what it is to be a person. This structuring of identity in intercultural terms can be seen as a deliberate act of mapping out a location from which to be and act out intercultural affiliations and cultural exclusions.

Discussion

Perhaps at the very heart of this study lies a desire to understand the strategic positioning of the "hybrid" self in different subject locations. Hence, our particular interests in the finding that these young females deliberately and strategically select different cultural identity markers, which they structure into different intercultural patterns of self-representation. The structurally intercultural singularity that each individual woman feels herself to be, is understood not as a substantive entity, but as a discursive intercultural location of the self: "[...] (a) site from which (to) perceive the world and [...] (a) place from which to act" (Harré, 1998).[10] One could postulate that these different structures incorporate a limited yet selected range of intercultural subject positions, each of which mobilises different sets of representations, knowledge structures, cognition, motivations and actions. It implies that these young females have the capacity to shift between circumscribed locations of intercultural identity, and to speak, as it were, from their different cultural centres of interest, emotion, thought and action.

It is this negotiation of the inclusion and exclusion of their different, relative, but unequal identities in a strategically structured intercultural representation of themselves, that points to the agency and intercultural embeddedness of the identity dynamics of these young, French-born females of African immigrant origins. In the light of the tensions and inequalities between reference cultures and the impossibility of satisfying their competing identity demands, interculturally structured identities are personalised strategies for mapping out a way of moving within and between cultures. This also involves being and acting in ways that fulfil each one's demands in part, or for part of the time. We have insisted all along that it is precisely by manipulating the insider-knowledge they possess about each culture, and shifting between different subject locations and intercultural sites of identity, that these young women bear witness to their agency in constructing their identities. They achieve this despite the constraining, undermining and discriminatory attributions made by others in their intercultural environments.

Conclusion

The outside world catches a glimpse of her changing at the street corner, from her deliberately tatty jeans or mini-skirt, to her tchador, removing all traces of the make-up belonging to the French face she shows at school. She then proceeds in the guise of an obedient and respectful young African woman, to her father's home—she takes on the appearance of a chameleon, playing off identities for her own benefit.

Her behaviour makes one wonder whom she really is, what she desires, values, or cherishes? But is this line of questioning appropriate? Does it not simply translate to our discomfort with her shifting location, our unwillingness to come to terms with the intercultural nature of her identity? We are stuck with the idea that it is in the in-between spaces of culture that she is to be found; that her identity is only shifting in so far as we insist on perceiving cultures as homogenous and bounded and identities as substantive.

If we were to stretch our imagination beyond the limits of cultural systems in contact, we could begin to conceptualise a third or "in-between" space, created by the intermingling of cultures, juxtaposed by tensions and brought closer by personal and group designs. Only then would we be poised to view this young woman's identity manoeuvres, not as shifting identities, but as an unfolding of an identity that spans the breadth of intercultural meanings and is captured and generated by its "in-betweens".

This chapter has sought to present a different perspective on gendered female African immigrant intercultural identity. We have focused neither on the internalised constraints imposed on female identity by affiliation to a patriarchal culture that conceptualises women in restrictive and oppressing terms, nor have we focused on the internalisation of negative, racially discriminating attributions made by a hegemonic host culture whose interest is vested in excluding these "hybrid" youths from accessing the privileges that accompany definition as "true" or "authentic" nationals. Rather, the chapter has insisted on the agency and intercultural embeddedness that characterises the negotiation and experience of identity among young women caught in the spaces between African immigrant and French host cultures.

Equipped with an understanding of each, these young women have been shown to actively select from each culture's reservoir a range of subject locations from which to be and act the different parts of their intercultural identities. In so doing, they assert their capacity to face up to the conflicting identity demands of each of their reference cultures, each of which competes for them to assume the gendered roles it construes as appropriate for a young woman of its own culture. It is this experience of straddling the tenuous divide between past and future meanings, that both colour the identity dynamics among these young women and open up new understandings for social scientists grappling with the puzzles presented by culture and identity.

In closing, one should perhaps draw attention to the fact that one limitation of an approach which focuses on the structures of identity, is that it does not sufficiently problematise the embodiment of these locations or sites by lived and experienced gendered subjectivities. The complexity of these women's identities can only truly be captured through a contextualised study. This context refers to the ways in which they live reality by inhabiting the spaces in ways that reflect their particular gendered experience. The latter refers to the experiences of being and acting as a woman from a national, ethnic, religious and racial subject perspective where tensions characterise the intercultural contact between their reference cultures. If we were to advance a hypothesis in this regard, it would be that these young women embody and experience the intercultural, as a site lived in and lived from, in an inclusive manner. In other words, we would presume that as women and as hybrids of doubled cultural consciousness, they would endeavour to include and give a voice to the largest possible number of their identity locations, rather than attempting to silence or exclude a part or parts thereof.

Notes

[1] Bakhtin. M. 1981. "Discourse in the novel", in Michael Holquist (Ed.), The Dialogic Imagination, translated by Caryl Emerson and Michael Holquist, Austin: University of Texas Press, p. 360, cited in Bhabha, H. 1996. "Cultures inbetween", in Stuart Hall and Paul Du Gay (eds), *Questions of Cultural Identity.* London: Sage Publications, p. 58.

[2] Suàrez-Orozco, C. and Suàrez-Orozco, M. 1996. "Latino Identities", in Lola Romanucci-Ross and George De Vos (eds), *Ethnic Identity: creation, conflict and accommodation.* Walnut Creek, CA: Altamira Press. pp.324-327.

[3] Suàrez-Orozco, C. and Suàrez-Orozco, M. 1995. *Transformations, Immigration, Family Life and Achievement Motivation among Latino Adolescents.* Stanford: Stanford University Press, cited in Suàrez-Orozco, C. and Suàrez-Orozco, M. 1996. "Latino Identities", in Lola Romanucci-Ross and George De Vos (Eds.) *Ethnic Identity: creation conflict and accommodation.* Walnut Creek, CA: Altamira Press. pp. 324-327.

[4] De Vos, G.A. 1973. *Socialization for Achievement: Essay on the Cultural Psychology of the Japanese.* Berkeley: University of California Press. Cited in Suàrez-Orozco, D. and Suàrez-Orozco, M. 1996. "Latino Identities", in Lola Romanucci-Ross and George De Vos (eds). *Ethnic Identity: Creation, Conflict and Accommodation.* Walnut Creek, CA: Altamira Press. p. 325.

[5] Eliot, T.S. 1949. *Notes Towards the Definition of Culture.* New York: Harcourt Brance. p. 62, cited in Bhabha, H. 1996. "Culture's in-between", in Stuart Hall and Paul Du Gay (eds). *Questions of Cultural Identity.* London: Sage Publications.

[6] Bhabha, H. 1996. "Culture's in-between", Stuart Hall and Paul Du Gay (eds). *Questions of Cultural Identity.* London: Sage Publications.

[7] Balibar, E. 1990. "Paradoxes of universality", in David Theo Goldberg (ed). *Anatomy of Racism.* Minneapolis and Oxford: University of Minnesota Press. p. 284, cited in Bhabha, H. 1996. "Culture's in-between", in Stuart Hall and Paul Du Gay (eds), *Questions of Cultural Identity.* London: Sage Publications.

[8] Camilleri, C. 1990. "Identité culturelle et gestion de la disparité culturelle: Essai d'une typologie". In: C. Camilleri, J. Kasterszein, M.E. Lipiansky, H. Malewska-Peyre, I. Taboada-Leonetti et A. Vasquez, *Stratégies identitaires.* Paris: PUF. pp.85-110.

Camilleri, C. 1994. "Enjeux, mécanismes et stratégies identitaires dans les contextes pluriculturels". In: *Les Hommes, leurs espaces et leurs aspirations. Hommages à Paul-Henri Chombart De Lauwe,* Paris: L'Harmattan. pp. 291-298

[9] For an example of a study dealing with the internalisation of negative stereotypes, see Vinsonneau, G. 1983. "Catégorisation et genèse de l'identité sociale: les jeunes Maghrébins en France". In: A. Bureau et D. De Saivre, *Apprentissages et cultures.* Paris: Karthala.

[10] Harré, R. 1998. *The Singular Self.* London: Sage Publications.

This chapter is part of Ph.D. research undertaken under the supervision of Anne Andronikof-Sanglade, Paris X. Nanterre, France.

We would like to thank the CSD-HSRC Pretoria and the French Foreign Ministry for their generous funding of this research.

References

Bakhtin, M. 1981. Discourse in the novel. In: Holquist, M. (ed.). *The dialogic imagination.* Trans. Emerson, C. & Holquist, M. Austin: University of Texas Press. pp. 360-347.

Balibar, E. 1990. Paradoxes of universality. In: Goldberg, D.T. (ed.). *Anatomy of racism.* Minneapolis and Oxford: University of Minnesota Press.

Bhabha, H. 1996. Culture's in-between. In: Hall, S. & Du Gay, P. (eds). *Questions of cultural identity.* London: Sage. pp. 53-60.

Camilleri, C. 1990. Identité culturelle et gestion de la disparité culturelle: Essai d'une typologie. In: Camilleri, C., Kasterszein, J., Lipiansky, M.E., Malewska-Peyre, H., Taboada-Leonetti, I. & Vasquez, A. *Stratégies identitaires.* Paris: PUF.

Camilleri, C. 1994. Enjeux, mécanismes et stratégies identitaires dans les contextes pluriculturels. In: *Les Hommes, leurs espaces et leurs aspirations. Hommages à Paul-Henri Chombart De Lauwe.* Paris: L'Harmattan.

De Vos, G.A. 1973. *Socialization for achievement: Essay on the cultural psychology of the Japanese.* Berkeley CA: University of California Press.

Eliot, T.S. 1949. *Notes towards the definition of culture.* New York: Harcourt Brace.

Harré, R. 1998. *The singular self* . London: Sage.

Suàrez-Orozco, C. & Suàrez-Orozco, M. 1995. *Transformations, immigration, family life and achievement motivation among Latino adolescents.* Stanford: Stanford University Press.

Suàrez-Orozco, C. & Suàrez-Orozco, M. 1996. "Latino identities". In: Romanucci-Ross, L. & De Vos, G. (eds.). *Ethnic identity: Creation, conflict and accommodation.* Walnut Creek CA.: Altamira Press.

Vinsonneau, G. 1983. Catégorisation et genèse de l'identité sociale: Les jeunes Maghrébins en France. In: Bureau, A. & De Saivre, D. *Apprentissages et cultures.* Paris: Karthala.

Chapter 8

Southern African Identity: A Critical Assessment

Ibbo Mandaza

Introduction

The subject of Southern African identity has to be considered against the background of a complex historical process that spans more than 300 years, and during which both Africa itself and Southern Africa in particular were moulded and shaped into geo-political *concepts* and *constructs*, after the image of an "expanding" and "conquering" Europe. It is a period characterised by *two contending world views*: the *Caucasian* one, on the basis of which contemporary Africa—and Southern Africa—have been defined, and remain largely intact today; and the *African nationalist* (or *Pan-Africanist*) identity, seeking to re-assert itself in the course of the struggle against European economic, social, cultural, racial and political domination. As this chapter will try to illustrate, the struggle between these contending world views remains largely unresolved. Instead, the struggle for the African recovery appears for the time being compromised by the enduring legacy of the *caucasian* world order.

African identity in general—and Southern African identity in particular—is necessarily a reflection of this historical transition. Against this background must be considered not only the historical, socio-economic bases of the key determinant of identity in Southern Africa—i.e. *race,* but also the issue of *class* and *ethnic* identity, including other derived identities, such as those of "colour". Therefore, it requires some focus on the nature and extent of the social engineering that characterised white racial domination—and *apartheid*—in Southern Africa; and an account of the complex interrelationship between race, colour and class identity in the Southern African context, including *ethnic* or "tribal" identification and *conflict*. The impact of all these factors on national situations—particularly the *National*

133

Question itself, and the problem of the (African) *nation-state-in-the-making*—is quite obvious and will receive brief mention. However, it is the main purpose of this chapter to assess so-called *Southern African identity* against the background of the two contending world views, in the context of the political economy of race, colour and class, and in relation to so-called *post-apartheid South Africa*. The problem of South African—or Southern African *exceptionalism*—will be presented as part of this identity crisis, as well as how this in turn impacts on the quest for regional co-operation and integration in both the Southern African sub-region itself, and in Africa generally.

The Caucasian world view and the political economy of race, ethnicity and class in Southern Africa

As has already been intimated, it was the *Caucasian* world view in terms of which Africa in general and Southern Africa in particular have been defined and developed as geo-political *concepts* or *constructs*. The following are the key elements in this historical process: the "European expansionism" which heralded the insertion of Africa into the international economic system, and began formally with the occupation of the Cape in 1652, in what thereby constituted the origins of this *Southern Africa*; the systematic conquest and wholesale destruction of African societies, particularly those of Southern Africa; the era of formal colonialism in the nineteenth century, particularly that given implicitly in the Cape-to-Cairo dream of British imperialist Cecil John Rhodes; and contemporary neo-colonialism, with its emphasis on the *continuity* of the colonial-type economy and the legacy of the post-colonial state.

To that extent, there is really nothing that is *Afrikan* about contemporary Africa, which is a *geo-political construct* that reflects more the image of those who made it over the 400 years or more that represent the continent's plunder and exploitation, than the *Afrika* that ought to have been recovered with post-colonialism. Indeed, if you look around us, there is little or nothing that is *Afrikan* about us: culturally, politically and economically, we are nothing but an appendage of Europe. What is *Afrikan* about the post-colonial state, when it is no more than a caretaker for those who govern our globe?

And what is so *Afrikan* about the post-colonial economy—if such a category does exist in these historical circumstances—when it is in reality a colonial-type one, exporting its raw materials for the industrial development of the northern hemisphere, and importing finished products to the detriment of its own industrialisation and employment opportunities? Indeed, what is *Afrikan* about the so-called *African middle class*, particularly that fraction of it that inherited (neo-colonial) power, when by its very nature it is largely *compradorian* and either *franco-phone*, *anglo-phone*, or *luso-phone*?

However, Southern Africa itself is a magnified version of this larger *geo-political concept* that is contemporary Africa. As a *geo-political construct* and *concept*, Southern Africa is no more than a reflection of the historical and socio-economic forces that almost succeeded in moulding it into a *White Dominion*. The colonialist agenda in Southern Africa was quite different from that which applied to the rest of Africa, in that implicitly, there was always the goal of creating *White Dominions* similar to those of Australia, Canada or New Zealand. Therefore, the logical expectations contained in such terms as the *Union of South Africa, Portuguese East Africa* (or *Portuguese Africa*, since Angola, Guinea Bissau and Mozambique were, in this colonial order, "provinces" of Portugal)—and the *self-governing colony of Southern Rhodesia*, not to mention the related attempt to extend the latter into the "Federation of Rhodesia and Nyasaland". Apartheid South Africa was, of course, an approximation of the *White Dominion* status; and the Unilateral Declaration of Independence (UDI) in "Rhodesia" was but a vain attempt at the same. In the end, it was *white Southern Africa* as a whole that sought to roll back the advance of the African nationalist struggle in Angola, Mozambique, Zimbabwe, Namibia and South Africa. There was also the intersection between the interests of white settler colonialism on the one hand, and those of a Western bloc and its Cold War imperatives on the other. This has to be borne in mind as a determining factor in the "historic compromises" that constituted a peculiar form of *decolonisation*, particularly in Zimbabwe, Namibia and South Africa.

Southern African identity or Southern African exceptionalism

Throughout the period of the Liberation Struggle, Southern Africa epitomised, in many respects, Africa's hope for recovery and restoration. This goal was best expressed by one of Africa's luminaries—Amilcar Cabral—in this period of the struggle:

> We are from the part of Africa which the imperialists call Black Africa. Yes, we are Black. But we are men like all other men. Our countries are economically backward. Our people are at a specific historical stage characterised by this backward condition of our economy. We must be conscious of this. We are African peoples, we have not invented many things, we do not possess today the special weapons which others possess, we have no big factories, we don't even have for our children the toys which other children have, but we do have our own hearts, our own heads, our own history. It is this history which the colonialists have taken from us. The colonialists usually say that it was they who brought us into history: today we show that this is not so. They made us leave history, our history, to follow them, right at the back, to follow the progress of their history. Today, in taking up arms to liberate ourselves, in following the example of other peoples who have taken up arms to liberate themselves, we want to return to our history, on our own feet, by our own means and through our own sacrifices.

The hope was that liberation itself would constitute a redefinition of Africa and Southern Africa; away from that geo-political concept to which reference was made in the introduction of this chapter—to one based on an *African identity* established through the resolution of the *National Question.* Prior to 1994, therefore, Southern Africa had a poignant meaning for those who identified with the struggle: it was a rallying call for all of Africa to rid itself of the last vestiges of colonialist domination. Therefore, there is a dual significance in the kind of "compromises" that the African nationalists have had to conclude with the former white settlers in Southern Africa. The first is obvious: that the agenda of the Liberation Struggle has not been fully realised and that decolonisation in Southern Africa has to be viewed not as the overnight event that was experienced throughout the rest of Africa, but as a difficult transition with many twists and turns, This is particularly so also because of the intersection between the historical and socio-economic exceptionalism of Southern Africa on the one hand, and, on the other, the global forces which have vested interests in their own continuity and are prepared to ensure that the new African states adhere to those rules and regulations of international capital. Hence the *constitutions* themselves are more than an expression of the *compromise;* they constitute the virtual guarantee—especially through the *Bill of Rights*—for (economic) *continuity,* in the maintenance of the old social relations of production, and even a "formal blessing" of the property ownership scheme that was established under white settler colonialism and *apartheid*. The only difference is that the "historically disadvantaged" can now all aspire to this new "meritocracy" while, in reality, it is only a lucky few who will make it.

Secondly, both the historical bases of Southern Africa and the "historic compromises" (made as part of this particular decolonisation process) account for the new kind of exceptionalism that is characteristic of the sub-region in general and South Africa in particular. It is an exceptionalist identity that turns history upside down: it is one not based on a critique of the incompleteness of the liberatory process; but on the contrary, an implicit attempt to extol it as the basis of a new vision—the *African Renaissance*—for the continent. This is part of the *new ideology of self-deception*, the refusal to acknowledge the current realities that parameter even our own political space as Africans—nationally, regionally and globally. As Jonathan Moyo has pointed out, the term *African Renaissance* poses the danger of masking realities in South Africa itself, while also speaking to a kind of exceptionalism that sets aside that country and the rest of the continent. Yet the attempt to *exceptionalise* South Africa is not so new. There was the old debate, in "white leftist" circles in particular, about "internal colonialism" or the implicit claim that South Africa was not a conventional "colonial case" and therefore not subject to the kind of decolonisation that had been attendant to most of Africa. Then there was the exceptionalism based on the sheer number of Whites, or even the temptation to make the latter the single most important factor in any political (or economic) calculation about the future of South Africa and Southern Africa. Indeed, it is difficult not to conclude that most of what has come to be in South Africa and Southern Africa is an outcome of such (racial) considerations.

Therefore, there is a real danger in this post-1994 period, of confusing *Southern African_identity* with the negative exceptionalism that is not only anti-Pan Africanist, but also a reflection of the preferential treatment that South Africa and Southern Africa receive from the international community, more often than not at the expense and disdain of the rest of the African continent. The point is that other Africans complain about this and cite it as one of the issues that undermines both interregional co-operation *and* the goal of African Unity. Clearly, South African and Southern African exceptionalism is one of the root causes of the conflict between the Southern African Development Community (SADC) and the Common Market for Eastern and Southern Africa (COMESA). This exceptionalism is therefore not confined to South Africa alone, even though it is most pronounced in that country. It is a Southern African disease: for example, before (post-apartheid) South Africa, Zimbabwe was just as guilty of this, with such neighbours as Botswana, Zambia and Malawi complaining about its dominance in the field of trade relations; and it is ironic now, that Zimbabwe herself should scream the loudest about South Africa's economic hegemony in the sub-region.

Toward a Southern African community?

The foregoing helps to highlight the constraints to regional co-operation and integration at both the sub-regional and continental levels. These constraints are broadly threefold, and are interrelated. First, there is the problem of vertical integration into the northern hemisphere. This is part of the historical and colonial legacy—reference to which was made at length in the opening paragraphs of this chapter. It expresses itself in the endless competition among African states for aid, access to markets, and even preferential treatment at the hands of elements in the northern hemisphere. This creates a "hierarchy of powers" at both the continental and sub-regional levels, undermining the potential for co-ordination and collaboration at the levels of interstate and inter-institutional processes. Secondly, there is the problem of uneven and unequal development within and between the African countries themselves, not to mention that between the sub-regional blocs-in-the-making. Among many other things, this complicates the process of trying to reconcile competing interests among member states, and renders difficult the task of joint mobilisation of resources for programme development. Thirdly, is the problem of the nation-state-in-the-making. Reference has already been made to this in the foregoing section of this chapter. However, the point to emphasise here is that unstable and insecure *nation-states* are inimical to the enterprise of regional cooperation and integration.

Therefore, it is far too early to speak of a *Southern African community*, let alone an organic *Southern African identity*. At worst, it is a double-faced identity: on the one hand, reflecting a sub-region defined in terms of the process of domination and colonisation; and, on the other, as an expression of intent, an ideology of a liberation struggle during which Southern Africa became a rallying call for the resolution of the *National Question*.

This is an ambivalence that can be resolved only in the context of renewed Pan Africanism; in the honest acknowledgement and genuine determination to confront the historical, political and economic factors that currently define Africa and Southern Africa; and in the realisation that the broader strategy and goal of African unity must prevail, carry and pervade both national and sub-regional efforts.

Chapter 9

Language Politics in South Africa

Neville Alexander

The following thoughts are an attempt at a programmatic level to develop my views on the relationship between language and identity in South Africa during the present phase of the consolidation of a liberal democratic polity. For the moment I shall simply take for granted that certain fundamental propositions relating to the whole question of identity construction are common cause among us. I append a recent article which I wrote for a non-academic readership in which I tried to summarise these core notions.

In South Africa, the major social markers of difference, i.e. "colour" or "race", language, "culture", gender, religion and region, as well as "class", have at different times played a decisive role—either alone or in some combination—as determinants of group or social identity. In recent times, however, regionalism has not been a major force for social mobilisation.

The chequered history of Afrikaner nationalism and its umbilical connection with racial oppression and separatism have left an enduring stigma on all language-based social movements in a country where the unity and coherence of the inherited colonial state is an article of faith, one that has a very real basis in the political economy of post-colonial Africa. Although the Organisation of African Unity is very tentatively beginning to reconsider its long-held view that the "artificial" borders of the modern states of Africa should be left as they are, this is still its treaty position.

In my first attempt at addressing the national question in South Africa in a systematic manner, I demonstrated the connection between the theories of nationality (or "ethnicity", as this is now called) held by the apartheid ideologues, and the development of the idea of "independent homelands" (NoSizwe, 1979). "Language", as defined by them, played the central role in their conceptualisation of the Bantu or Black "nations" which they, in their own terms, were guiding to "independent statehood". This historical fact has meant that for most of the post-war generation of black—as well as progressive intellectuals and activists generally— language-based social movements were suspect. Such movements were routinely dismissed or condemned as "tribalist". The reception originally accorded the Inkatha Cultural Movement in these circles, for example, is ample evidence of this assertion.

Even within the rigidities of the apartheid ideological grid, however, there were many contradictions. Of these, the most blatant were the fact that in that framework, "white" South Africans constituted a "nation" in spite of the fact that they were composed of at least two language communities, whereas "black" South Africans were identified and categorised in terms of so-called "language groups". Within these, again, two "Xhosa" nations were accommodated. The particular reasons for these inconsistencies are no doubt very interesting, but not relevant in the present context.

More relevant is the fact that for decades, Stalin's theory of the nation had a very strong influence among political activists in regard to their notions of nation building and the evolution of the nation in South Africa. Since that theory postulated "a common language" as one of the necessary attributes of a nation, it tended, ironically, to entrench, on the one hand, the middle-class notion that under South African conditions the universalisation of the English language was an essential precondition for the building of a modern nation in this country. Before the accession to power of the Afrikaner National Party in 1948, on the other hand, there were, especially in the ranks of the Communist Party of South Africa, many activists who believed that Stalin's ideas on this question meant that the different "tribal" (now "ethnic") languages could or should constitute the basis for the creation of different African nations in Southern Africa. These would eventually be united in a Federation of Soviet Socialist Republics (NoSizwe, 1979; Alexander, 1986). After 1948, of course, this approach represented the kiss of death to any political programme that hoped to find a positive response among the masses of the African people.

As against these historical positions, the African National Congress (ANC), the Non-European Unity Movement (NEUM) and the Pan-Africanist Congress (PAC) as well as the Black Consciousness Movement (BCM) somewhat later, in practice pursued a nation-building strategy that was based on the assumption that nations are not necessarily monolingual. Indeed, the NEUM, in its relevant documents explicitly rejected the Stalinist prescriptions in this regard. All of these political formations objectively considered language communities to be valid sub-national identities. In other words, they espoused the construction of a national (South African or Azanian) identity and accepted that people would also identify themselves (or be identified as) Afrikaans-, Zulu-, Xhosa-, Tswana-speaking, etc., and that this was a completely normal phenomenon in any modern industrial state.

The practice of these organised political forces had many implications and contradictions. I have drawn attention to one of the main ones in some of my recent writings on the language question. I refer to the fact that in reality, all of these formations pursued an "English-only" or an "English-mainly" policy, thereby contributing to the hegemony of English in South Africa. In my view, because of the "class" position of their leadership, they were unable to arrive at a programme of action on the language question that would be consonant with the promotion of the interests of their social base, viz, the urban and the rural poor. The vast majority of these people did not speak or even understand English. At levels of empowering proficiency, only middle-class people in South Africa can be said to speak English. Yet, there was no thought of systematically encouraging and helping people to learn one another's languages on a significant scale. There was no equivalent to the kind of literacy and other cultural programmes started by the Afrikaner nationalists after the Anglo-Boer War. A cultural-political strategy that consequentially pursued the objective of facilitating communication among the masses of South Africa's workers in town and country, was never, as far as I am aware, even proposed. In my view, this was one of the most important mistakes of progressive political leadership in the South African movement, and I refer especially to the left-wing elements in the movement. Eddie Roux and others attempted to promote English literacy, and the Night-School Associations certainly managed to spread the knowledge of reading and writing in some of the African languages, but all these efforts remained sporadic and none of them, in any case, was conceptualised as part and parcel of a larger cultural-political programme along the lines that Amilcar Cabral, for example, pursued for Guinea-Bissau.

This is the reason why there continues to be tension between the explicit constitutionally enshrined principles of the promotion of multilingualism in South Africa, and the concurrent practical commitment to the hegemonic status of English— among all South African politicians, except among the right and the left wings. For very different reasons, these two groups of activists are opposed to policies that effectively render the urban and the rural poor silent, voiceless and disempowered. Again, the details of this particular irony might be very interesting but they do not have to be explored in greater detail for the purposes of my argument.

On paper, we have now made the paradigm shift from the conception of the monolingual to that of the multilingual nation. This is, among other things, the historic import of the new constitution. In practice, however, most people are quite confused as to the practical meaning of this shift. Indeed, the fatal concession that was made to the Freedom Front (FF) on the question of religious, cultural and linguistic communities, indicates that the full significance of the commitment to multilingualism was not understood by the fathers and the mothers of the nation. Elsewhere (Alexander, in James & Maharaj, 1998). I have shown that this concession represents the beginning of the formal "ethnicisation" of politics in post-apartheid South Africa. Everything that has happened in the recent past demonstrates that this is in fact the danger we are facing. Lest I be misunderstood, let me state clearly that I am not opposed to identities constructed on the basis of linguistic affiliation as long as these are clearly sub-national in character and tendency. For political as well as philosophical reasons this seems to me to be the wisest position to adopt. Anything else infallibly leads to the oppression of one group by another. The concessions made to General Viljoen and his party, however, bear within themselves the seeds of the destruction of the South African polity as we know it. The setting up of a separatist dynamic in South African politics, via the politicisation of the language question, i.e., the intersection of economic and power-political interests with language differences among the people, is an ever-present possibility. Hence it is crucial that the political and cultural leadership of the country recognise that the language question has to be treated consciously and consistently within the paradigm of the multilingual nation. Otherwise, we shall fall into the trap that John Saul revealed in the early eighties in his seminal article on "the dialectics of class and tribe".

Already, we have the purported leaders of all kinds of "language communities" knocking at the door of the Pan South African Language Board (PANSALB), asking for recognition of their speech varieties as "official languages". In some cases, at least, the link between these requests and access to monetary and other resources, is quite obvious. (For a not dissimilar situation, see Mahmood Mamdani's recent description of the ethnic dynamic in Nigeria (Mamdani, 1998).) Hitherto, we have been spared the spectacle of language-based political parties appealing for votes to their alleged constituencies. This is so only because perceived racial issues are still the most salient ones in this society. But that can change very rapidly, especially if anti-racist strategies are effective.

In general, the salience of the racial factor in South African politics has indeed worked against the construction of language-based group identities that could be or have been politically mobilised. The cases of white Afrikaans-speaking people and, with many more qualifications, of black Zulu-speaking people, are exceptions that have proven the rule. It seems to me, therefore, that we have to take great care not to create frames of reference that will facilitate the political mobilisation of language communities in South Africa. It is essential that we conceptualise the existing and evolving language communities as tributaries of a Gariep nation constituted by many other tributaries that originate in linguistic, religious and other cultural and regional catchment areas. All together constitute the mainstream of the South African or Azanian nation. In the present era of globalising flux which has as its dialectical counterpart the generation of local (from village to continental) footholds of stability, it is very important that we understand the fluid relationship between global, national, sub-national group and individual identities. One can do this without falling into the total relativism which some post-modernist discourses seem to imply. This is a relationship that requires much more exploration, reflection and debate, and it is one which we, in South Africa, should begin to take seriously, so that we head off any possibility of our country slipping into the abyss of tribal/ethnic warfare in future.

A few words are necessary about the *lingua-franca* status of English in South Africa. Given the fact that English has, during the past 50 years or so, become not merely *a* but in fact, *the* global language (Crystal, 1997), as well as the fact that South Africa has an entrenched English orientation because of colonial conquest, it would be merely quixotic were one to suggest that the English language should be downgraded in this country. English, it is widely agreed, is the *lingua franca* of the middle classes and of the intelligentsia in South Africa. There is no doubt that for the foreseeable future this situation will remain unchanged. Moreover it is clear that the fact that the present governing *elites* are able to communicate with one another across the barriers of colour and language by means of this bridging language, is critically important for the smooth running of public administration, and for decision making more generally. However, even at this level, it must be understood that first-language speakers as well as "co-ordinate bilinguals" who use English, are at a distinct advantage, as against those for whom English is a second or even a third language. This is one reason why a policy of multilingualism should be promoted in tandem with the promotion of English as the *lingua franca* for the entire population. For, and this is the crucial point: unless all South Africans have reasonable access to English so that all of them—including the urban and the rural poor—have the possibility of becoming proficient in the language, we will do no more than to perpetuate the *de facto* post-colonial language policy of the rest of the African continent, a policy that has failed at every level (Prah, 1995).

That policy, as Pierre Alexandre (1972) pointed out more than two decades ago, transforms English (in this case) into a form of cultural "capital" by means of which the middle-class *elites* reinforce their power over their compatriots. This is already happening in South Africa. Unless the Pan South African Language Board and other language-planning agencies begin to operate effectively, the almost ideal framework for a democratic language policy which is embedded within the new constitution, will remain a dead letter—and a historic opportunity will have been wasted. Retracing our steps some 30 or 40 years "later", as is now happening in many other African countries, will be extremely difficult and demoralising. Indeed, I would go as far as to say that it might already have become impossible. Instead of looking at some version of the Swiss model, we might then be staring at the disastrous wasteland of a kind of ex-Yugoslavia.

References

Alexander, N. 1986. Approaches to the national question in South Africa. *Transformation*, 1(1).

Alexander, N. 1998. *Language and the national question in South Africa*. In: James, W. & Maharaj, G. *South Africa between unity and diversity*. Cape Town: IDASA.

Alexandre, P. 1972. *Language and languages in Africa*. London: Heinemann.

Crystal, D. 1997. *English as a global language*. Cambridge: Cambridge University Press.

Mamdani, M. 1998. Now is the time to squeeze Lagos junta. *The Sunday Independent*. 14 June.

NoSizwe, 1979. *One Azania one nation. The national question in South Africa*. London: Zed Press.

Prah, K. 1995. *Mother tongue for scientific and technological development in Africa*. Bonn: Deutsche Stiftung für Internationale Entwicklung.

APPENDIX

New identities for old

All people want to belong to a larger social unit; all of us seek a "comfort zone" which, in the best of all possible worlds, is usually conceived of as an extension of the family. Today, when the family has become a very problematic entity in most urban contexts, the same sense of belonging and security is sought, and often found, in other associations or "in-groups", ranging from religious communities to all manner of clubs. I do not have the space to trace here the psychological structures and mechanisms that are at play from before the birth of the individual, and by means of which s/he acquires various identities. It is enough to state clearly that all human beings need, as part of their survival kit, an ideological envelope, as it were, from within which they perceive and experience the world. How that envelope gets constructed is very much a matter of time, place and circumstances and necessarily differs from one individual to the next (even as between identical twins).

Identities are socially constructed. That means we are not born with an "identity", even though we may be predisposed by the circumstances of birth to assume a specific identity. Someone born into a Xhosa-speaking family is, all other things remaining the same, very likely to identify broadly with other Xhosa-speaking people. But, if by some accident the person were to be removed from the family within the first few months or years after birth, and grew up in a different linguistic environment, s/he will assume a quite different identity. This crude reference to time, place and circumstance ought to get us away from the mystique which extreme nationalists and other romantics graft onto the concept of identity ("Germans are born, not bred", and similar notions of primordial or divinely ordained identities).

We never have only one identity. All of us have multiple identities, i.e. we identify in different degrees with many different groups. For example, we may "feel at home" within a particular language group but the people who constitute that language community, in all probability, all belong to different churches (in the Christian context). Afrikaans-speaking people, for example, may belong to the DRC, the Roman Catholic, the Methodist, etc., churches, and a minority adhere to one or other Islamic community. If we look at the same language community from the point of view of what sports teams they identify with, we would arrive at any number ranging from the local to the provincial and the national and different types of sports within those levels. In other words, identities are *situationally* determined and there is a hierarchy of such identities which each individual assumes. Under certain circumstances and for certain purposes, one identity will be more important to the individual than another; being Afrikaans speaking may be less important in the context of a visit to Rome for a member of the Roman Catholic community, for example.

We are most often "given" identities by others who act on the basis of stereotypes they have internalised. In a racially structured society such as South Africa, having a dark skin and being Afrikaans speaking, will almost certainly earn you the label "coloured", whether you like it or not. Any South African knows the infinite variety of such stereotypes in terms of which we classify and categorise fellow South Africans. These stereotypes are a kind of museum of past social categories. For this reason, ascribed identities are the most difficult to change. They represent in many different ways the stable, consolidated "social universe" of the dominant groups in a society. For, it is in the ideology of these groups that others are "placed" in their respective social categories or identities. It was, for example, the Dutch East India Company that decided who was a Dutchman, a slave, or a Khoi, etc. While the subordinate groups are not completely without influence on how they are stereotyped, the decisive categorising power lies with the dominant group or groups. It is in their interests that the social hierarchy (castes, classes, "races", gender categories, language groups, etc.) is established, and it is in their interests to keep it that way.

Identities are, therefore, contested. The categories, "coloured" and "bantu", to take but two recent examples, were (and are) rejected by many and even most of the people so labelled. This rejection is part of the larger social struggle for equality, freedom, dignity and fair access to the resources of the country. Whether or not a particular identity is mobilised politically depends on many circumstances. Most often, the markers of identity such as language, colour, religion, region, are seized upon by ethnic entrepreneurs in order to use the energy and the power of the mobilised people for the purpose of gaining political and/or economic advantage. What has to be guarded against is the opportunistic and usually charlatan attempts to invent or to reinvent identities by power-seeking or aspiring *elites* who see the chance of catching the votes of their "captive audience". In the larger continental context, this phenomenon has given rise to devastating ethnic conflicts, and in post-colonial Africa, debilitating ethnic fragmentation.

In South Africa today we are faced with a situation that calls for rapid and often dramatic shifts in identity or, in some cases, for the consolidation of inherited identities. To mention only a few: the categories "African", "Afrikaner", "Coloured", "Zulu", amongst others, are being hotly contested. While this might sometimes resemble a game of words, it is a deadly serious game, the outcome of which may make the difference between decades of peace or war. The notion of the "rainbow nation" generated in a fit of excitement by Archbishop Tutu, is an attempt to gloss over the contradictions that characterise post-apartheid South Africa. The illusion of coherence and unity which it is intended to convey, dissipates at the first touch of the bitter reality of racial, class and caste divisions.

There is little point in trying to analyse the particular metaphor of the rainbow, but metaphors are powerful instruments of mobilisation and conscientisation, as every advertising agency will tell you. My own objections to the "rainbow" stem from the fact that its immediate source is the very different social and historical context of the U.S.A., on the one hand, and, on the other hand, that it highlights the question of colour and of groups conceived of as coexisting colour- or "racial" groups. Since the first critical voices were raised, there have been many other kinds of objections raised, but any metaphor can be analysed to death and I shall not get into that game here.

As an alternative, I have proposed the metaphor of the Gariep, i.e., the Great River. This has numerous advantages in terms of describing the dynamic and the real variability or diversity of our society as it is structured at present. The image presents itself because of the historical fact that South African society, as we know it, has come about through the flowing together—mostly violently, sometimes in a relatively peaceful manner—of three main "tributaries"—carrying different cultural traditions, practices, customs, beliefs, etc. These currents or streams are the African, the European and the Asian. Today, we have to add, as most countries in the world have to do, the modern American, or "coca-cola", stream.

It is an indigenous image. The Gariep (Orange River) is one of the major geographical features of this country. It traverses the whole of South Africa and its tributaries have their catchment areas in all parts of the country. It is also a dynamic metaphor, which gets us away from the sense of unchanging, eternal and god-given identities. For this reason, it is appropriate for the transitional period in which we are living. It accommodates the fact that at certain times of our history, any one tributary might flow more strongly than the others, that new streamlets and springs come into being and add their drops to this or that tributary, even as others dry up and disappear; above all, it represents the decisive notion that the mainstream is constituted by the confluence of all the tributaries, i.e., that no single current dominates, that all the tributaries in their ever-changing forms continue to exist as such, even as they continue to constitute and reconstitute the mainstream.

This is very different from the notions of multicultural societies prevalent in Europe, North America and Australia—where a *main* stream (the Anglo-Saxon or the German, etc.) dominates while it "tolerates" the coexistence of other (minority) cultures. In view of the present debate about our "Africanness", this is an important way of seeing what we are trying to capture through the images and metaphors we use to express our intentions and our orientation.

Concretely, my position means that we have to accept that identities in South Africa today are subject to rapid change; we have to open

151

windows onto one another, allow as much mutual influence to happen as possible; we have to get away from treating any identity as though it is like some irremoveable skin without which we would be disfigured. We have to begin to see it more as an inescapable mask which can be changed as we acquire new knowledge or interests. In spite of the passions that are so easily inflamed when this or that "sacred" practice or belief is questioned, we have to begin to understand that what we want to bring about in the new South Africa is a cultural domain without boundaries. The notion of discrete "cultures", by which apartheid was justified, is a reactionary notion which cuts people off from one another, undermines any sense of national unity and deepens the prejudices and negative stereotypes we have inherited from our colonial and apartheid past.

In my view our primary identity should be that of "being South African", not in any exclusivist or national-chauvinist sense. The fact is that as long as the national state is the political and economic entity in terms of which international relations are structured, even if only on the surface, this identity is an inescapable one. Any other identities we assume should not undermine this sense of being South African. Finally, we have to become much more conscious of the stereotypes we carry around with us as being so much racial and ethnic baggage that makes it difficult, and even impossible for us to connect with fellow South Africans and fellow Africans.

These views are necessarily stated in abridged form. They are meant to stimulate discussion and to open the way for the serious business of positioning ourselves in a post-modern world where much has become uncertain and much more has become possible.

Chapter 10

Shifting African Identities: The Boundaries of Ethnicity and Religion in Africa's Experience

Ali A. Mazrui

Among the most serious consequences of colonial rule and racial domination are the crises of identity which they generate. The old assurances of long-established traditional identities are suddenly shaken. Established values are questioned and foundations of legitimacy are eroded.

Additional complications arise when the colonial order implants, encourages or even invents whole new identities. In most parts of Africa there was no such thing as a Christian identity before the arrival of the white man and his cultural baggage. Christianisation was not only the propagation of a new religion, it was also the creation of a new identity in sharp contrast to, say, African Muslim identity or traditional religious identity.

The colonial order also created new "tribes", either by splitting a big one into smaller ones (as when the Batoro were separated away from the Banyoro in Uganda), or by uniting groups which had previously been distinct (as in the creation of the concept of Yoruba identity, to encompass previously separate kingdoms).

Many of the ethnic groups of Africa are, in the final analysis, linguistic groupings. What is a Yoruba? One possible answer is: "A person to whom the Yoruba language is the mother tongue." What is a Shona? A similar answer is possible for the Shona, as it is for the Wolof, the Zulu, the Kikuyu, the Amhara, and the Baganda. Language is usually a necessary condition for ethnic difference in Africa, but never a sufficient condition. African "tribes" differ in more than just language, but language is often central to their cosmology and world view.

There was a time when it was widely assumed that the learning of *European* languages would be a detribalising experience for Africans. Westernisation might have eroded many African traditional *practices*, but it has not eroded ethnic *loyalties*. In some cases ethnic rivalries have intensified rather than diminished in response to Westernising influences.

This chapter is in part about those ethnic forces. But ethnicity does not act in isolation. It interacts with such additional social forces as the rural-urban divide, the underlying class struggle, the social dialectic between men and women, and the impact of religion on society.

The two most powerful primordial forces operating in Africa are indeed *ethnicity* and *religion*. Ethnicity defines the basic social order; religion defines the basic sacred order. Ethnicity creates the solidarity of shared identity; religion creates the solidarity of shared beliefs.

In the context of sub-Saharan Africa, the word *ethnicity* is used to replace the old concept of "tribe". In Africa south of the Sahara, there may be 1 500 to 2 000 ethnic groups. Arab Africa is more homogenous outside the Sudan. In Arab Africa north of the Sudan, the smaller ethnic groups include the Nubi, the Berbers, and in a religio-cultural sense, the Copts.

While ethnic *groups* in Africa number in their hundreds, it is arguable that there are only three religious *traditions*—the indigenous, the Islamic and the Christian. The religions of the different ethnic groups are much more similar than their languages. It is therefore possible to conceptualise their sacred beliefs as constituting one single religious tradition—the indigenous legacy.

If there are hundreds of ethnic groups, and only three basic religious traditions in Africa, one is tempted to conclude that ethnicity in Africa is a divisive force while religion is potentially unifying—especially since the other two religious traditions in Africa, Christianity and Islam, are worldwide fraternities. Christianity and Islam are also doctrinally universalist.

This chapter will explore the relationship between ethnicity, religion and the balance between unity and fragmentation in Africa. How do such primordial forces affect contemporary politics and the struggle for national and regional integration? Let us look more closely at the interplay between primordiality and statecraft, between religion and ethnicity, between domestic forces and international repercussions.

Parochial religion and transnational ethnicity

At one level Christianity and Islam are indeed universalistic religions; and this should therefore have the effect of transnationalising the politics of its adherents in Africa. Muslims of one African country, for example, should find areas of political solidarity with Muslims in another African country.

Ethnicity (in the sense of "tribalism"), on the other hand, appears to be a case of sub-national identity. It should therefore be a parochialising force rather than a transnationalising tendency in Africa.

But there are occasions in Africa's experience when the roles of religion and ethnicity are reversed. In such situations it is ethnicity which becomes a transnational and Pan-African force—while Christianity and Islam become parochialising and fragmenting to the nation.

The most dramatic recent case of transnational ethnicity has been the impact of the Tutsi on the whole area of the Great Lakes in Africa. The Rwanda Tutsi who were in exile in Uganda, formed an army of their own and became the *Rwanda Patriotic Front.*

As exiled Tutsi they staged their own "Bay of Pigs" operation into Rwanda in 1994. This was in the middle of the Hutu genocide against the Tutsi in Rwanda, following the shooting down of the presidential plane in April 1994.

The Rwanda Patriotic Front from Uganda entered Rwanda not to perpetrate carnage but to pursue conquest. With remarkable discipline they resisted the temptation of committing countergenocide against the Hutu. Instead, they went for the capital city, Kigale, and succeeded in capturing it. To all intents and purposes, their triumphant "Bay of Pigs" Operation established a new Tutsi-led political order in Rwanda.

Two years later, the indigenous Tutsi of Zaire (as it was then called) were being harassed by the authorities and the armed forces of Zaire. The local Tutsi were being treated as if they were immigrants from Rwanda, when in fact they were indigenous to Zaire. The Tutsi of Zaire decided to resist—and proceeded to form a fighting force. To their surprise they were militarily successful against the official security forces of Zaire. The victory whetted the appetite of the resisters—and a wider rebellion against the Mobutu regime in Zaire was born.

As the rebellion gathered momentum, it attracted more and more of the discontented groups of Zaire to join it. More significantly, it attracted Laurent Kabila, originally from Shaba province of Zaire. Kabila captured the leadership of the movement from then on, culminating in the capture of the capital city, Kinshasa, in May-June 1997. Kabila then became President of the renamed *Democratic Republic of Congo*.

Earlier, Yoweri Museveni—and Museveni was a Muhima, Ugandan Tutsi by another name—captured power in Uganda in 1986. Ethnically he was from the Bahima, close ethnic cousins of the Tutsi. The exiled Rwandans in Uganda had helped him capture power. After 1986 it was "pay-back time".

He wanted to help exiled Rwandans find their way back home. Museveni, as a Ugandan "Tutsi", helped to create the *Rwanda Patriotic Front* which then captured power in Rwanda. The new configuration of the Rwanda-Uganda coalition helped the Tutsi of Zaire to start a rebellion which culminated in the overthrow of the 32-year-old dictatorship of Mobutu Sese Seko in distant Kinshasa.

What this story of the Great Lakes since 1994 has revealed, is that Pan-Tutsiism can be a *transnational* force. It has helped to change the history of Uganda, Rwanda *and* the new Democratic Republic of Congo quite significantly. This is quite apart from the unsettled role of the Tutsi of Burundi, a country which is still profoundly divided against itself.

Ethnicity *within* countries, between the Hutu and the Tutsi continues to be a horrendous and bloody experience. But Pan-Tutsiism, as a solidarity movement, demonstrates that it can also be a region-wide liberalising force. Uganda, Rwanda and Zaire have moved closer to liberalisation than they were before the Tutsi-Hima factors helped to transform them, and when in 1998 Kabila (now assassinated and succeeded by his son) turned for a while against his Tutsi benefactors, conflict in the Congo rapidly ignored borders once again.

Certainly the rebellions against Mobutu Sese Seko and later Kabila, were neither purely national nor indeed exclusively ethnic. The rebellions against Mobutu and Kabila were region-wide and almost pan-African. In addition to help from Rwanda and Uganda, the conflicts also involved other countries for example Angola, though the ethnic configurations here were different.

The conclusion to be drawn from all this is that ethnicity in Africa is not only a fragmenting force within countries; it can also become a transitional or supra-national force linking one country to another.

Paradoxically Christianity and Islam are sometimes *parochialising* forces in Africa. This has certainly been the case in Nigeria (Africa's largest country in terms of population) and Sudan (Africa's largest country in terms of territory).

In Nigeria almost all Hausa are Muslims; almost all Igbo are Christians; and the Yoruba are split between Christians and Muslims. Islam has reinforced Hausa identity and its differentiation from non-Muslim groups; Christianity has reinforced Igbo identity and its differentiation from non-Christian groups.

It seems almost certain therefore that the Hausa would have felt less "different" from their non-Muslim neighbours had the Hausa never been Islamised. And perhaps the Igbo would have felt less culturally "superior" to their neighbours had the Igbo never been Christianised by Europeans.

The conclusion to be drawn, is that Christianity and Islam, although universalist religions in doctrine and proselytising ambition, have had parochialising consequences in certain African situations.

This is certainly also the case in Sudan where the fact that the southern region is basically non-Muslim has sharpened its differentiation from the more Islamised and Arabised north. The fact that the southern political leaders have been disproportionately drawn from the small Christianised minority within the south has contributed further towards deepening the cleavage between north and south. Once again Islam and Christianity—far from creating "universalist bonds" among people—have only resulted in aggravating regional and ethnic sectionalism.

Models of church-state relationships

On the relationship between church and state considered institutionally, the African experience has approximated four models. One model is that of *theocracy*—in which an African country has an established church-state and church institutions have been interlocked. Ethiopia, before the revolution of 1974 was, to all intents and purposes, such a Christian theocracy. The imperial monarchy traced its origins to King Solomon of the Jews and had links with the Ethiopian Orthodox Church. Nearly half the population of Ethiopia was not Christians at all. This sharpened the distinction between Christian Ethiopia, on one side, and Muslim and traditionalist Ethiopia, on the other.

Sudan, since 1983, has been another kind of theocracy—this time an Islamic theocracy. It began with the Presidency of Ja'afar Numeriry, who attempted to base the Sudan's legal order upon the Shari'a (the Islamic law). Numeriry was overthrown in the wake of popular demonstrations in 1985, and Sudan even experimented briefly with a revived multiparty system with Sadeq el-Mahdi as Prime Minister. But the Islamic laws (the so-called September laws) were not abolished. When the military returned to power under General Umar Hassan Ahmad Al-Bashir, the Sudanese state moved even more deeply into Islamisation. This process also resulted in sharper differentiation between Northern and Southern Sudan.

Another model of the relationship between religion and politics in Africa is based on the concept of a religious *nation* rather than a religious *state*. While Ethiopia before 1974, and Sudan since 1983, were *religious states*, Zambia in the 1990s officially declared itself a religious *nation*. With effect from President Frederick Chiluba's presidency, Zambia is officially a "Christian nation".

Ironically, President Chiluba's predecessor as Head of State, Kenneth Kaunda, was in many ways a more religious figure than Chiluba, and was descended from a more clerical family, but Kenneth Kaunda preferred to stick to the concepts of both a secular nation and a secular state. However, Chiluba's declaration of Zambia as officially a "Christian nation" immediately marginalised the millions of followers of African traditional religions and followers of syncretic movements. It also marginalised the one million Muslims and the thousands of followers of the religions of South Asia (such as Hinduism). Once again Christianising had the effect of narrow-mindedness and parochialisation.

On the other hand, Chiluba's declaration of Zambia as a "Christian nation" has attracted more Western militant evangelical missionaries— sometimes even at the expense of the older Anglican and Catholic traditions of Zambia. Here too, Christianity proved to be a fragmenting rather than universalising force.

The third model of relationship between religion and politics in Africa is that of the *ecumenical state*. In this case there is neither a state religion, nor is the state completely separate from religious institutions. What distinguishes an ecumenical state is its readiness to accommodate the different religions through official institutions or through official processes, or both.

Outside Africa, Lebanon is the ecumenical state *par excellence*. There the entire constitutional order is based on power-sharing among the different religious denominations. The President is a Maronite Christian; the Prime Minister, a Shiite Muslim; the Speaker of the House has to be a Sunni, and the seats of the legislature are allocated according to the different denominations.

In Uganda in the 1970s President Idi Amin Dada experimented with the ecumenical state, within which the government was supposed to be the arbiter and referee between Catholics, Protestants and Muslims. But Idi Amin's Uganda was, in other respects, too disorderly and tyrannical to accomplish a credible ecumenical state.

A *de facto* ecumenical state is Senegal. Its population is 94% Muslim—a greater percentage than the Muslim population of Egypt. Yet, in the first 20 years of its independence, Muslim Senegal had a Roman Catholic president—Leopold Sedar Senghor. Among African countries Senegal is a relatively open society. President Senghor had many political opponents who called him such names as "lackey of France", "political prostitute", "hypocrite of Negritude". What the critics seldom called him was *kafir*, or infidel. In other words, his religion was almost never held against him. Leopold Senghor had worked out a special relationship with the *Marabouts* and other religious leaders of Muslim Senegal. The political process was *de facto* ecumenical.

To comprehend the scale of the Senegalese achievement, we need to compare it with the record of the United States. Although the United States has been a secular state for two centuries, it has only once strayed away from the Protestant fraternity in relation to the Presidency. We are not even sure that Catholic John F. Kennedy had indeed won the majority of the popular vote, especially since there was some "hanky-panky" in the balloting in Illinois. But whatever the electoral figures, Kennedy did become the first and only Roman Catholic President of the United States.

American Jews have done extremely well in the country and have penetrated every institution of power to some extent or another. But American Jews have not even tried to capture the White House. They have wisely decided that a Jewish candidate for the Presidency could provoke so much Christian fundamentalism and anti-Semitism that they would lose the gains they have made as a community in terms of influence and power since the end of World War II. The Jews have left the U.S. presidency alone.

Now there are as many Muslims as Jews in the United States. A Muslim President of the United States is still a mind-boggling prospect in this constitutionally secular state. And yet little Senegal had a Christian president in an overwhelmingly Muslim society. Today Senegal does have a Muslim President—Abdou Diouf—new president in Senegal. Yet the First Lady is Roman Catholic. How many Western politicians would make it to the position of Head of Government or Head of State if their spouses were Muslim?

What all this means, is that Senegal has developed a *de facto* ecumenical state long before any Western country approached such a degree of religious broadmindedness.

Malawi seems to have a Christian majority. Yet in 1994, Malawi elected its first Muslim president—another case of African liberalism in sharp contrast to the West. But Malawi cannot really be described as an ecumenical state, since there are no interlocking arrangements between the state and religious leaders as there are in Senegal. However, Malawi could be described as a more convincingly *secular state* at the level of the presidency than almost all Western countries. No Western state is capable of electing a Muslim president or prime minister in the foreseeable future (except in such Muslim-majority countries as Bosnia, Albania and Turkey).

Tanzania seems to be a half-way house between a secular state and an ecumenical state. Without any constitutional stipulation, the country seems to be leaning towards a system of *religious alternation* of the presidency. It began with a Christian president (Julius K. Nyerere). He was succeeded by a Muslim president (Ali Hassan Mwinyi) who in turn has now been succeeded by another Christian president (Benjamin Mkapa). It seems very likely that the first president of the 21st century will once again be a Muslim. Tanzania's stability will be at risk if that does not happen.

What all this means is that the fourth model of relationship between religion and politics in Africa, is indeed *the secular state*—but sometimes more complex, and sometimes more genuinely secular—than anything achieved in the western world. The great majority of African states do try to be secular—but combine this with a readiness to accommodate not only *ethnic arithmetic* (a quantified balance between ethnic groups) but also *the sacred calculus* (a compromise with the demographics of religion).

The secular state of Sierra Leone elected its first Muslim president in 1996—President Ahmed Tejan Kabba. His government was overthrown in a military *coup* in May 1997. Muslim-led Nigeria offered to intervene militarily in Sierra Leone to restore the democratically elected government to power. Was the Nigerian government acting on behalf of the Economic Organisation of West African States (ECOWAS) in this military venture?

It seemed strange that a military government like that of Nigeria should seek to defend democracy in another country. Yet Africa has experienced exactly opposite situations before—Western democracies seeking to defend military dictatorships in Africa. If one had a choice, it is better to see a military regime defending democracy (as in the case of Nigeria and Sierra Leone) than to see a democracy defend a military government (as the United States and France had often done in the past in defending Mobutu Sese Seko's military government).

The struggle continues in Africa—to contain ethnicity as a sub-national force, without neutralising its potential as a Pan-African supra-national force.

The triple heritage of religion in Africa is alive and well—indigenous, Islamic and Christian. What is often overlooked is that the indigenous religious forces are the most ecumenical—promoting the spirit of "live and let live" in the spiritual [and political?] domain.

Parochial ethnicity and transnationalising religion

The reverse situation of ethnicity as internally divisive—and religion as transnationally unifying—has also been part and parcel of the African experience. Indeed, Sub-Saharan Africa's worst civil wars have been fundamentally ethnic—including the Nigerian civil war (1967-1970); the war for independence of Eritrea (1962-1992), and the Angolan civil war (1974 into the 1990s).

On the other hand, conflicts in North Africa have tended to be religiously inspired rather than ethnically focused. This includes the civil war in Algeria, which has been going on since the military aborted the 1992 elections to prevent an electoral victory by the Islamists (the Islamic Salvation Front). By the middle of 1997, over 60 000 people had been killed in the dirty and indiscriminate Algerian conflict.

Also religiously focused, is political violence in Egypt—at two levels—the struggle of the Islamists against the pro-Western government of President Husni Mubarak, and in favour of a more Islamically oriented Egypt; and secondly, the tension between Muslims and the minority Coptic Christian Church.

If civil wars in North Africa are mainly religiously inspired and civil wars in sub-Saharan Africa are mainly ethnically inspired, Sudan once again falls in-between, exhibiting features of both ethnicity and sectarianism.

The fundamental divide between Northern Sudan and Southern Sudan is ethnic and cultural—but this ethno-cultural divide has been reinforced by the fact that the North is much more Arabised and Islamised, and the South is partially Christianised. In this and many other respects, the Sudan illustrates the contradictions of both Arab Africa and Sub-Saharan Black Africa.

The religious aspect of the Sudanese conflict had international consequences. In the first Sudanese civil war (1955-1972), the Southern side successfully presented itself internationally as a victim of an Islamic *Jihad* from the North. Efforts of the Khartoum government to promote and teach the Arabic language in the South were portrayed as efforts at forced conversion to Islam. Government take-over of missionary schools (which has been happening all over Africa regardless of religion) was condemned as a strategy of Islamisation.

In reality the Sudanese government's policy in the South—from 1955—was an attempt at national integration through a *language* policy rather than a religious policy. The idea was to integrate and develop the South through the Arabic language (the most widely spoken language in the country) rather than continuing with the primacy of the English language as a medium of instruction, as most Christian missionary schools had chosen to do.

But the wider world seldom drew any sharp distinction between a language policy of Arabicisation and a religious policy of Islamisation. So the first Sudanese civil war was widely regarded as a religious confrontation between a Muslim government in Khartoum and its armies, and Christian liberation fighters in the South. Fortunately, negotiations in Addis Ababa in 1972 were at last successful in bringing that particular conflict to an end.

It was the second Sudanese civil war which began in 1983, which was more clearly provoked by a new *religious* policy of Islamisation from Khartoum. Beginning with the regime of General Ja'far Numeiry, and later sustained more thoroughly by the Government of General Umar Hassan Ahmad Al-Bashir, as well as the ideological leadership of Hassan Turabi, Sudanese regimes attempted to construct an Islamic state. The religious policy became transnationalised when the Sudan in the 1990s saw itself as an international revolutionary force, and supported liberation movements elsewhere. Sudan's critics saw its Islamic regime as a supporter of international terrorism.

More purely ethnic conflicts elsewhere in Africa were also tempted sometimes to use the religious card, either to win support for themselves or to demonise their enemy. The population of Eritrea is a mixture of Christians and Muslims. But sometimes in the course of Eritrea's war for independence, the Islamic card was used to win support from the Arabs in Eritrea's struggle—first against the Christian theocracy of Haile Selassie, and later against the Marxist-Leninist atheism of Mangistu Haile-Mariam in Addis Ababa.

In their struggle to create the separate state of Biafra, the Igbo of eastern Nigeria often used the religious card to win sympathy for themselves as "Christians" and to demonise the Federal Government of Nigeria as "Muslim-dominated". The Biafran propagandists often tried to portray the North-South divide in Nigeria as a Muslim-Christian divide. Such a characterisation of the North-South divide was a distortion—but it was a good propaganda ploy in the competition for support in the western world.

When Idi Amin (a Muslim) was in power in Uganda (1971 to 1979), the ethnic strife in the country was often externally portrayed as Muslim *versus* Christian struggles. In reality, those conflicts were fundamentally "tribalistic"—Kakwa versus Acholi; Nubi versus Langi; Nilotics versus Bantu; the Baganda against their rivals.

On the other hand Idi Amin's expulsion of Israelis from Uganda in 1972 did win him many friends in the Arab world. Indeed, Amin's break of diplomatic relations with Israel a year before the 1973 October war in the Middle East made him a path-breaker in the new Afro-Arab solidarity against Zionism. Idi Amin set a precedent for Africa's break with Israel in 1972—which was followed by almost every other African state the following year, in the wake of the October war.

A pro-Arab orientation in Idi Amin's foreign policy from 1972 onwards was one of the few consistent aspects of his regime. The Arab world was not ungrateful. Libyan troops briefly tried to save him when the Tanzanian army invaded Uganda in 1979—and then the Libyans decided to go neutral after a while. Tripoli and later Riyadh gave Idi Amin comfortable political asylum with his entourage after he was ousted from power by Tanzanian troops in 1979. Idi Amin is still a guest of the Royal Saudi House.

Domestically the convulsions within Amin's Uganda were indeed mainly ethnic, regional and "tribalistic". The religious divide was third or fourth in importance. But in foreign policy, the Islamic factor was more important than it was domestically. From 1972 onwards, Idi Amin's foreign policy was increasingly influenced by Pan-Islamic considerations.

The nature of the civil conflicts within Africa may in turn be categorised as either politically primary or politically secondary. A politically primary civil war, for example, is one which seeks to redefine the boundaries of the political community. Civil wars which are secessionist or fundamentally separatist, are politically primary in this sense. The Nigerian Civil War (in which the Igbo tried to create an independent Biafra) was therefore politically primary. It sought to redefine the boundaries of the political community. This is also true of the 30-year war for the independence of Eritrea (1962-1992).

On the other hand, the 1997 conflict in Zaire (now Congo) led by the late Laurent Kabila was basically *secondary*. The ideals and goals of the Kabila movement were not separatist. The goal was to capture power in Kinshasa and create a better political order.

The civil war in Mozambique—while it lasted—was also basically secondary, since it entailed no major secessionist or separatist tendencies. It was at best a clash of ideologies and personalities. A *secondary civil war* is concerned not with changing the *boundaries* of the political community, but with redefining the *goals* of the political community, or enlisting new *leadership*.

Sudan has had two such phases. The first Sudanese civil war, with the Anya Nya in the South (1955-1972), was fundamentally secessionist and was therefore primary. It concerned the boundaries of the political community. The second Sudanese civil war (from 1983 onwards), was led by the rebellion of John Garang in the South. Garang was not after the separatist ideal of a new country of the South. He was after helping to democratise and secularise Sudan as a whole. The second Sudanese civil war has been, on the whole, *secondary* in nature since 1983 (in spite of the presence of a few individual secessionists both North and South).

South Africa: The racial war that never was

There was a time when South Africa seemed destined to experience one of the bloodiest examples of *primary* civil wars—an actual racial war appeared inevitable. After all, everywhere else in Africa where there had been a large white minority, there had been severe bloodshed before full majority rule was realised. Kenya experienced the Mau Mau war (1952-1960); Algeria experienced its war of independence (1954-1962); and Rhodesia and Angola had their equivalent conflicts. Since South Africa had the largest white minority of them all, how could South Africa possibly avert the same bloodstained fate?

One particular difference turned out to be more relevant than many people imagined. The Whites of South Africa identified themselves with Africa, but not with the Africans. The Afrikaners especially were passionately loyal to the African soil (the land) but not loyal to the African blood (the indigenous people).

In contrast, the Whites of colonial Algeria were loyal neither to Africa nor to the Africans. Their loyalty was to France. They owed no special allegiance to the soil of Africa except as a means of livelihood. They certainly owed no loyalty to the blood of the indigenous peoples. They attempted to turn Africa into an extension of France.

Similarly, the Whites of Angola attempted to turn their part of Africa into an extension of Portugal. This is in contrast to those Whites in South Africa who identified themselves with the African soil so much that they called themselves Afrikaners, and even attempted to monopolise the name "*Africans*" for themselves.

White Rhodesians were simply too British, many of them enjoying dual citizenship right through Ian Smith's Unilateral Declaration of Independence (UDI). Of all the Whites of Africa, perhaps only the Afrikaners had evolved a mystical relationship to the African land. The Afrikaners mixed their sweat mystically with the African soil, but did not mix their blood spiritually with the African people.

How did South Africa avert a racial war in the twentieth century? One reason was indeed cultural—this was the simple fact that the Afrikaners were half-way towards Africanisation through a marriage between the Afrikaner *soul* and the African *soil.*

A second reason why South Africa has averted a racial war in the twentieth century is essentially a division of labour between black political power and white economic privilege. The white man said to the black man: "You take the crown, and I will keep the jewels!" The black man was to acquire the political crown, while the white man retained the economic jewels. In many ways, while political apartheid was ending, economic apartheid is still intact. The best land, the best mines, the best jobs, the best shops and commercial opportunities, are still over-whelmingly in white hands or under white control. The challenge for the post-Mandela South Africa is how to dismantle economic apartheid without causing widespread economic and social havoc.

While most people are convinced that South Africa has indeed averted a primary civil war in the twentieth century (White versus Black), can we be complacent about averting it in the 21st century if economic apartheid remains intact? The 21st century may not have the moral leadership of the rank of Nelson Mandela. It may still have the valuable resource of the marriage between the Afrikaner soul and the African soil.

But this brings us to the third reason why South Africa has averted a racial war in the 20th century. This concerns Africa's short memory of hate. Cultures vary considerably in their hate retention. The Irish have high retention of memories of atrocities perpetrated by the English. The Armenians have long memories about atrocities committed against them by the Turks in the Ottoman Empire. The Jews have long memories about their martyrdom in history.

On the other hand Jomo Kenyatta proceeded to forgive his British tormentors very soon after being released from unjust imprisonment. He even published a book entitled *Suffering without bitterness.* Where but in Africa could somebody like Ian Smith, who had unleashed a war which killed many thousands of black people, remain free after black majority rule—to torment his black successors in power whose policies had killed far fewer people than Ian Smith's policies had done?

Nelson Mandela lost 27 of the best years of his life. Yet on being released he was not only in favour of reconciliation between Blacks and Whites. He went to beg white terrorists who were fasting unto death, not to do so. He went out of his way to go and pay his respects to Mrs Verwoerd, the widow of the architect of apartheid. Is Africa's short memory of hate sometimes "too short"?

What saved South Africa from a primary civil war in the 20th century? It was a convergence of those three forces: The mystical relationship between the Afrikaner soul and the African soil, the Black African's short memory of hate, and the historic bargain which conceded the political crown to Blacks and kept the economic jewels for Whites in at least the 20th century.

Political violence: Primary and secondary

The distinction between primary conflict (boundaries of a political community) and secondary (goals of a political community), is not necessarily a measure of the violence generated by either. Yes, we do start from the premise that a civil war which is a battle about breaking up a country (like the American civil war of the 1860s) is more fundamental than a civil war about which ideology prevails or which leaders triumph (like the Spanish civil war of the 1930s). And yet it is possible for a secondary civil war about ideology and "*who rules*", to generate much more violence than the dispute over whether a country survives as one entity.

The worst case of genocide in Africa occurred in Rwanda in 1994. And yet the Hutu-Tutsi confrontation in Rwanda and Burundi has almost never been about secession—it has much more often been about who rules. The genocide of Rwanda in 1994 was, in our terms, a case of *secondary* political violence, however horrendous we may deem its scale.

The civil war of the 1990s in Algeria is "secondary" in our sense, since it is neither secessionist nor separatist in any sense. But the Algerian war has been internationalised in a big way. The violence in Algeria has spilt over into France, partly because the Government in Paris has been perceived as being supportive of the anti-Islamist regime in Algiers. And because the borders of the European Union are now more fluid and open to nationals of its member countries, violence involving Algerians in France has become a matter of concern to France's European neighbours as well.

Algeria's own Arab neighbours fear a different kind of spill-over effect—not the spread of direct Algerian violence (as has happened in Paris) but the spread of politicised Islam among Moroccans, Tunisians and other North Africans. Morocco and Tunisia especially fear the "contagion effect" of militant Islam in their own populations.

Just as the Algerian war of independence (1954-1962) had a greater impact on Europe than any other African anti-colonial war, so Algeria's confrontation between militant Islam and militarised secularism may be pregnant with implications for France and Europe as a whole.

The Algerian war of independence changed the course of French history in a number of decisive ways. It put so much stress on the French political system between 1954 and 1958, that France itself hovered on the brink of a civil war in 1958. Only one man could save the situation— Charles de Gaulle, who was persuaded to emerge from retirement in a new hour of crisis. The Algerian war—and Charles de Gaulle between them— convinced France at long last that the Fourth Republic was not working. The Fifth Republic was born after a referendum. Because the Algerian war had helped to give birth to the Fifth French Republic, it ironically helped to give French governments greater stability under the new Constitution. Because the Algerian crisis had helped to bring Charles de Gaulle back into power, the impact on European and world history was wide ranging.

Under De Gaulle, France pulled out of the military wing of the North Atlantic Treaty Organisation (NATO); France kept Great Britain out of the European Economic Community for the rest of the 1960s; France more vigorously pursued an independent nuclear military policy; and France gave political independence to almost all its African colonies within two or three years of De Gaulle's assumption of power. Algeria itself became independent in 1962.

If the Algerian war of independence was so multifaceted in its impact on Europe and the world, will the Algerian civil war of the 1990s also turn out to be pivotal internationally? The war is certainly being watched closely in a wide array of capitals of the world.

While the big universalising issue of the war of independence was the dilemma between Algerian self-determination and French sovereignty, the big universalising issue of the civil war in the 1990s is the dilemma between the dream of an Islamic democracy (aborted in 1992 by the military), and the rival dream of a liberal secular democracy (preferred by the secular political parties of Algeria).

With regard to the two religious struggles in Egypt in the 1990s, one is clearly secondary and the other is semi-primary. The struggle of the Islamists to replace Husni Mubarak with an Islamic constitutional order is secondary in our sense, since no separatist or secessionist issues are involved. However, the tension between Islamic militants and the Copts has features that are semi-primary since the tensions often imply profound unhappiness about Copts and Muslims being citizens of the same country. Of course most Egyptians are religiously tolerant and would "live and let live". But there are extremists among both Muslims and Copts who regard it as a tragedy that they share the same country. It is in that sense that this particular religious tension in Egypt is semi-primary, and culturally "separatist".

Of the two Egyptian struggles, the secondary one against Husni Mubarak, has had wider international ramifications. While the Algerian Islamist struggle has spilled over into France, the Egyptian Islamist struggle has spilled over into the United States. Rightly or wrongly, some have even seen a direct connection between Islamist threats to Nobel Laureate Neguib Mahfuz in Egypt, on one side, and the blowing up of the World Trade Center in the United States, on the other. Political violence in Egypt evolves into political terrorism in the United States, according to this view.

Once again it is hard to draw a sharp line, separating religion as a divisive force domestically, from religion as an international force in world affairs.

The seven pillars of the African Renaissance

In 1994 I was invited to a conference at the Central State University in Wilberforce, Ohio. There was one big condition imposed on paper-writers for this conference. No papers which were pessimistic about the African condition would be allowed.

This was a conference for *Afro-optimists*—not for Afro-pessimists! I accepted the condition. I wrote a paper entitled "AFRENAISSANCE" (one word), prefixing the letters "Af" before the word "renaissance".

If I had known that the term "African Renaissance" was going to be so popular in Southern Africa a few years later, I would have insisted on the immediate publication of my paper. Unfortunately I gave the English language rights of my paper to Central State University who have been in negotiation with Stanford University Press about publishing the whole proceedings. They are taking their time.

Until August 1998, the only published proof in existence that I had even written such a paper, was in *German*. My paper was translated and published in 1996 in the German journal *International Politik* (Bonn), Volume 51, No. 9. In August 1998 there was further proof that such a paper existed. The German version became an entry in the bibliography, *The Mazruiana Collection,* compiled by Abdul S. Bemath (New Delhi: Sterling Publishers; and Johannesburg: Foundation for Global Dialogue, 1998).

The Renaissance in the history of Europe was a return to the Greco-Roman Classics that followed the Middle Ages. The European Renaissance was partly a liberation from the heavy hand of Christianity (imported from the Middle East) and an attempt to recover the spontaneity of ancient Greece at its best.

Afrenaissance—or the Renaissance in Africa—must also be, in part, a "return" to the classics. And what is a return to the African classics? It must involve a partial return to African culture and civilisation. The African Renaissance must in part involve the *re-Africanisation* of Africa—based on seven principles.

If both ethnicity and religion are primordial forces, how do they relate to the African Renaissance? What is *primordial,* is in many respects a compact with the past. What constitutes a *renaissance,* implies a new life altogether, rather than mere revivalism or revitalisation. A renaissance is more than a resurrection of the old life—it is a re-birth of a new life.

Yet the European Renaissance—while it lasted—was, as we indicated, a return to the classics of Greece and Rome and a retreat from the dogmatic world of medieval Christianity. Similarly, the African Renaissance has to be, in part, a reaching back to the authenticity of the ancestors.

Africa has a triple heritage of religion—indigenous, Islamic and Christian. Without the African Renaissance, the most disadvantaged religious tradition in Africa was likely to remain the indigenous one. Most members of the African *elítes* regarded African traditional religion with condescension, often dismissing it as "superstition".

The African Renaissance would therefore hopefully restore parity of esteem among Africa's three religious traditions—thus raising indigenous beliefs to the same level as Christianity and Islam. On the other hand, Christianity and Islam—in the era of the African Renaissance—have to allow themselves to be significantly Africanised if they are to survive vibrantly in the new Africa. (This is the *religious imperative.*)

Another force in Afrenaissance, is language. The African Renaissance requires a new recognition of, and respect for indigenous African languages. South Africa has made a start in recognising 11 official languages, though the country has yet to spell out what that recognition means in practice. We know that the new policy has put Afrikaans on the defensive. Should it continue to be ranked alongside English as a national language? Or should Afrikaans be ranked alongside Zulu and Xhosa as one more African "vernacular" in the broad South African configuration?

In relation to identity, language does pose agonising dilemmas. Will promoting multiple African languages activate ethnicity? Or will it consolidate a sense of Africanity?

All over Africa, new language policies are needed which pay greater attention to indigenous languages in schools and other societal institutions, while cautioning against the negative aspects of ethnicity. The African Renaissance should include university degrees in African languages continent-wide, and newspapers in African languages from Maputo to Maiduguri. In time, law making itself will have to be in African languages. (This is the *language imperative*.)

A third force in Afrenaissance is the role of oral and indigenous history. We need to confront some of the perennial prejudices which have in the past reduced Africans to the status of a people without a history. Afrenaissance demands a review of African history and of the methods of studying it. Change is needed in the direction of restoring Africa to its rightful place in global history. (This is the *history imperative,* often deeply related to issues of identity.)

But in the contemporary world, Africa has been left behind partly because its own skills and talents have been denied opportunities for growth and development. The colonial educational system has been culturally alien and often ineffective in bringing out the best in young Africans. The graduates of these colonial institutions have constituted *elítes* of leisure, rather than *elítes* of labour, exemplars of western tastes, rather than of western skills. The African Renaissance needs to overhaul not only educational institutions, but also systems of inducements and rewards, not least in relations between men and women. African talents lie among both genders, and they all need to be given a new lease on life—the African genius needs to be re-awakened. (This is the *talent imperative*.)

Once this talent has been reactivated, Africans may be able to give new meaning to self-development and self-reliance in a real partnership between men and women. Instead of stagnant economies and marginal technologies, the continent may be able to look forward to a new millennium of self-sustaining achievement. (This is the *imperative of self-development.)*

But man does not live by yam or corn alone. Afrenaissance should aim not just for prosperity but also for humane governance and clean self-rule. Would humane governance require some kind of "democracy"? Does "clean self-rule" imply an individualism and a multiparty system? How much female empowerment is the absolute minimum Africa can tolerate? Afrenaissance will let each African country evolve its own optimum institutions of humane political order. (This is the imperative of *humane self-governance*.)

The seventh pillar of the African Renaissance moves from the local to the global level. This seventh pillar combines the old struggle for human dignity with the new realities of globalisation. The forces of globalisation should not be allowed to undermine recognition of Africanity as a dignified face of humanity. Afrenaissance is, in part, a creative African response to globalisation and related historic trends. (This is the imperative of *humane globalisation*.)

Conclusion

We have sought to explore in this chapter, the complex relationship between Africa's two most powerful primordial forces—religion and ethnicity—and how they have affected the political process. Of particular interest to this discussion has been the balance between integration and fragmentation, and between domestic forces and international repercussions.

Most Africanist scholarship has examined politicised ethnicity in Africa as a problem for national integration. This chapter has raised the question of whether ethnicity is sometimes unifying—region-wide.

On the other hand, there are assumptions in the popular mind about the universalism of either Christianity or Islam, or both. This chapter has raised the question as to whether Christianity and Islam can sometimes be parochialising forces. If so, under what circumstances?

Over-simplifying observers tend to divide the world into countries that are secular and countries that have an established church. This chapter has discussed the third category of the *ecumenical* state in Africa—sometimes displaying greater religious liberalism (as in Senegal) than the West has as yet achieved. Senegal is a Muslim country which accepted a Roman Catholic President for 20 years (1960-1980).

This chapter has also distinguished primary civil wars (disputing the *boundaries* of the political community) from secondary civil wars (disputing the *goals* or *leadership* of the political community). Countries that are torn by a primary civil war are probably at a lower level of national integration than countries that are quarrelling about *goals* or "who rules".

However the scale of violence is not necessarily commensurate with the distinction between primary and secondary. In the single year of 1994 more people died in small Rwanda (a secondary civil war) than died in three years of civil war (1967-1970) in Nigeria, which had nearly 15 times the population of Rwanda. Yet the Nigerian civil war (with a lower casualty rate) was secessionist and therefore primary.

The complexities of Africa's social and political experience continue to unfold. An African miracle of ending political apartheid in South Africa has arrived. Primordial forces of race, ethnicity and religion intersect with processes of new identity-formation and enlargement of political scale. Out of such tumult and anguish, out of tension and tribulation, a new face of Africa is bound to emerge—bruised, but hopefully unbowed.

An African Renaissance is feasible, provided it is built on the seven pillars of sustainability. Has the process of Afrenaissance begun?

Index